What a Novel Idea!

What a Novel Idea!

Projects and Activities for Young Adult Literature

Katherine Wiesolek Kuta

1997
TEACHER IDEAS PRESS
Libraries Unlimited
A Division of Greenwood Publishing Group, Inc.
Westport, Connecticut

TEACHER IDEAS PRESS
Libraries Unlimited
A Division of Greenwood Publishing Group, Inc.
88 Post Road West
Westport, CT 06881
1-800-225-5800
www.lu.com/tip

Production Editor: Stephen Haenel
Copy Editor: Aviva Rothschild
Proofreader: Lori Kranz
Typesetter: Michael Florman

Library of Congress Cataloging-in-Publication Data

Kuta, Katherine Wiesolek, 1952-
    What a novel idea! : projects and activities for young adult
  literature / Katherine Wiesolek Kuta.
    xi, 143 p. 22x28 cm.
    ISBN 1-56308-479-1
    1. Young adult literature--Study and teaching--Activity programs.
  2. Young adults--Books and reading--Activity programs. I. Title.
PN1009.A1K88 1997
809'.89283'07--dc21   97-279
                                                            CIP

DEDICATION

*This book is dedicated to several
special people who helped me
tremendously in many ways.*

*My daughter, Melanie, who loves books at three
and is proud of her mother being a teacher.*

*My husband, Tom, who understands
what giving time to others means
and has been a strong support during the writing of this book.*

*My mom, who read to me
and encouraged me to pursue all my dreams and endeavors.*

*My colleague Donna Stupple, who has assisted me with computer technology
and has answered my never-ending questions.*

*All my students who have been my critics
and have been willing to read, to take risks with these projects,
and to grow as individuals.*

Contents

PREFACE

The purpose of this book is to provide activities and projects for teachers to use with their students as before, during, and/or after reading activities with young adult literature, particularly novels. Certainly this resource book could be used for authentic assessment because all the activity projects involve students' performance in displaying their knowledge and understanding of a book in a creative, original manner. Students could work on these projects in groups, pairs, or individually as directed by the teacher.

This book offers 60 activities and projects of a wide range that can accommodate several different learning styles. Some students prefer activities that require reading and writing if they tend to be skillful in these areas. Other students prefer creating objects that show and represent their knowledge. Those students who tend to be very verbal may feel most comfortable with speaking to an audience in a small or large setting for their project. Teachers should offer choice and variety to accommodate students' interests whenever possible, but all students should be exposed to all modes of expression and skills.

Most of these activities can be adapted for any grade level, ability group, type of class, or type of literature. Because the teacher's purpose for assigning an activity may vary as do the skills that need reinforcing, the activities are divided into three parts, with 20 activity projects in each section, that emphasize two of the six reading/English standards: reading, writing, representing, viewing, speaking, and listening. All six skills may be required in some way for any particular project.

The criteria used for selection of the material were based on successful classroom-tested projects. Most of the activities I have used myself with students. Many teachers have shared their ideas with me over my 22 years of teaching in the classroom. I have taught in several Chicago area school districts ranging from kindergarten through college, and I have found that high school students were the most challenging and the most enjoyable. They need the opportunity to express themselves individually, to be successful and increase self-esteem, and to learn about themselves and the world they live in. One means of doing all of the above is through young adult literature and activity projects.

Through my experiences, I have become acquainted with many professional teachers who were kind enough to share ideas with me. These ideas have been saved, changed, and molded to fit my needs and the needs of the students that I was working with at any one time. I am thankful to all my colleagues who have shared ideas and materials with me when I was "the new kid on the block" during the years of starting over with a new class, grade level, or school. This book has now allowed me to organize the old as well as create the new so that I can share successful materials with others.

I have taught remedial students during my entire teaching career, and there are three things I have found that add to success with students. One is to plan a variety of activities for use within a class. The second is to give students the power of choice, and the third suggestion is to use young adult literature in the classroom. These have been my most successful motivating factors that have worked well with all my students. I wrote this book with these three factors constantly in mind.

Because teachers like ready-made materials that meet their needs, the activities and projects are reproducible. Each activity project has a list of purposes, how to use the activity, evaluation, and variations. Teachers can change or enlarge the forms as they feel necessary.

I hope that you as an educator become more enriched with ideas by using this book with your students and that your students learn to grow to be lifelong readers.

INTRODUCTION

With the publication of the International Reading Association and the National Council of Teachers of English's *Standards for English/Reading Language Arts* in 1996, I felt a need to show teachers the kinds of activities and projects that are already being done successfully in the classroom that match the standards that are explained in the document. These six necessary skill standards—reading, writing, representing, viewing, speaking, and listening—are stated more specifically in the 12 student-centered standards recently published.

The emphasis in the English/reading classroom is for students to develop and grow to the best of their ability by providing opportunities for them to increase their skills and become more literate in the world as citizens who are readers, writers, and speakers. This book offers students opportunities in all six areas.

The first part concentrates on reading and writing activity projects. The projects include writing essays, news stories, letters, summaries, fiction, and creative responses. These projects have been grouped together because the students are involved in not only reading a work of literature but also having a writing experience concerned with that book. These activities are not in any particular order since a teacher could choose a specific activity to meet a specific purpose or several activities could be offered to students to choose among for a project.

The second part deals with activities and projects that offer students the opportunity to display their knowledge of a book in the form of visuals, such as a chart or artwork. Even in this part, the students must read a piece of literature and there may be some writing involved in the project, but the focus is on the information being represented in an unusual, creative format as requested in the individual activity project. Some of the formats may include a collage, poster, mobile, mural, bumper sticker, bookmark, or greeting card. The second phase of the project is sharing the creation with the class members for their viewing. Students need to take responsibility for their learning by sharing and learning from one another. This cooperation enables the teacher to act as a facilitator in the classroom. The use of the visual becomes a teaching device for students to use during presentations whether it be formally or informally.

The third part of the book offers activities and projects for students to practice the speaking and listening standards. The activities were designed for students to use verbal skills and not only be creative in some instances, but also present orally to the class or small groups. Some activities include a one-minute booktalk, panel discussion, interview, oral book review, and an oral presentation of a passage. The class members get to practice their listening skills as they become the audience for the presentations.

For all 60 activity projects, there is an explanation sheet that gives the teacher pertinent information on the purposes of the activity, how to use the activity, evaluation points, and variations for uses with the activity. All 60 activity projects are reproducible and ready to use in the classroom. The variety in the activities should make this resource book a useful tool to increase students' participation, motivation, and assessment.

Reading and Writing
Standards Activities

ACTIVITY 1

CHARACTER ANALYSIS

Purpose of the Activity

The purpose of this activity is to involve students as active readers. They will be writing and taking notes about a character as they read the text. Students will also reflect on whether they think the character is likable or not based on the information they have in front of them. Students will use the information on this graphic organizer, a visual structure that displays information, to make a one- to three-sentence conclusion on whether or not a character is likable with an explanation of their reasons.

How to Use the Activity

Use this activity with students during reading, starting at the beginning of the reading. Most of the information about main characters appears during the exposition of the novel, which generally comprises the first couple of chapters of the book. Students can learn about exposition and character development by charting information on this form. This activity can be assigned to individuals, pairs, or groups. Use this form as a model with a short work first to ensure understanding.

Evaluation

How the activity is used determines the evaluation and credit for the assignment. One possibility is to give credit for completion of this activity as well as separate credit for sharing with a partner or the class. Hopefully, as students become more careful readers, they will be able to monitor their own understanding of a character and realize that in a novel the author gives pertinent information during the exposition of the plot to develop the characters as real people.

Variations

After students gain understanding of the main character's development, use this form and ask students to trace the development of other characters as they are introduced throughout the book. You can also have students draw symbols that represent each character's personality, and this activity can lead to further discussion and understanding of each person.

ACTIVITY 1

CHARACTER ANALYSIS

Name: _____ Date: _____

Title: _____

Author: _____

Publisher and year: _____

Directions: Choose a main character from your novel whom you would like to get to know better as a person. We learn about people by what they say, how they act, and what others tell us; we also learn about characters in books this way. You will keep track of one character and write down information about this person as you read about him or her. Make sure to include page numbers and specific examples.

Physical Description

1._____

2._____

3._____

4._____

5._____

Personality Description

1._____

2._____

3._____

4._____

5._____

NAME OF CHARACTER

Background Information

1._____

2._____

3._____

4._____

5._____

Problems in Life

1._____

2._____

3._____

4._____

5._____

On the back of this sheet, write one to three sentences to explain why this character is likable or not.

From *What a Novel Idea!* © 1997 Katherine Wiesolek Kuta. Teacher Ideas Press. 1-800-237-6124.

ACTIVITY 2

PROFILE OF MAIN CHARACTER'S PERSONALITY

Purpose of the Activity

The purpose of this activity is for students to look for specific information, to draw inferences, and to understand the main character's personality. The students will practice moving beyond the text as they read or after completion of the reading to gain greater understanding of people and themselves.

How to Use the Activity

This activity can be assigned during or after reading. Before the activity is assigned, however, have the students practice it on themselves. Ask the students to create a circle out of their own paper and cover half the circle with another color paper or color in half the circle. Then ask the students to write several of their own personality traits that are obvious to everyone in class. For the darker side of the circle, students can think of a couple of their traits that only special friends or family know about. Discussion and information sharing would help students understand themselves, each other, and the activity for the main character. Students need to take notes on a character as the author relates information throughout the text. As they read, they must look for less-obvious traits based on a character's decisions, conversation, and behavior. This will help them be more perceptive readers.

Evaluation

Assess this activity in terms of how well the students understand the main character by using specific examples from the novel. If the activity is used as a class activity, student participation should be taken into consideration.

Variations

This activity can be expanded on in several ways to increase depth and understanding. One possibility is to assign a variety of characters to different groups of students and have group members decide which personality traits are the most important ones to share with the class. Also, after a discussion, a game can be created to match characters with personality traits.

ACTIVITY 2

PROFILE OF MAIN CHARACTER'S PERSONALITY

Name: _____ Date: _____

Title: _____

Author: _____

Publisher and year: _____

Everyone has obvious personality traits, parts of themselves that are easily seen by everyone else. Each person also has a hidden side that is not shown to anyone except good friends or parents. Choose an important character from the novel and find three to five external personality traits that are stated by the author directly through description. Then look for three to five internal personality traits that first are learned by the reader through a character's words, actions, or behavior throughout the novel. Label them in the correct side of the circle.

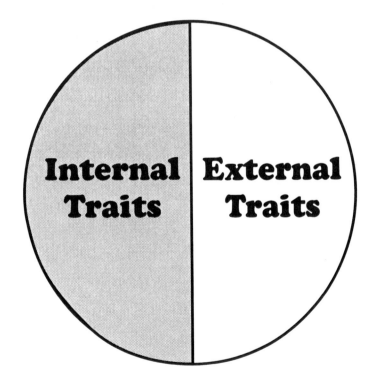

CHARACTER'S NAME _____

INTERNAL TRAITS   **EXTERNAL TRAITS**

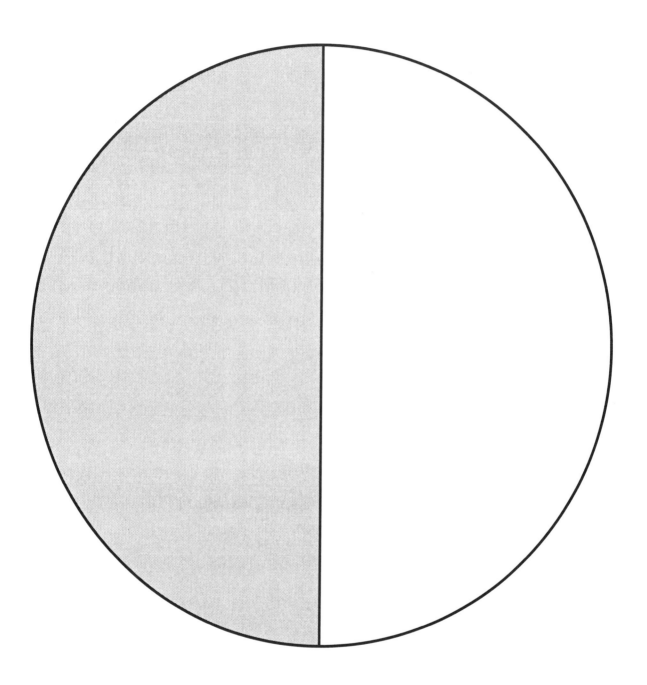

ACTIVITY 3

ELEMENTS OF FICTION CHART

Purpose of the Activity

This reading and writing activity is designed to help students understand the important parts of a story as well as the whole novel that they are reading or have completed. The activity can be used during or after reading. The goal is for students to look for these elements of fiction when they are reading independently.

How to Use the Activity

This activity should probably be used in three phases. The first phase should consist of teaching through direct instruction, modeling by showing students how to complete the task, and controlling the discussion of the terms and responses.

Using a children's book, short story, or easy novel would be ideal to help students become familiar with the form and terms. The first column can be used for definitions of the terms. The second phase should consist of group discussion responses, and the second column can be used for these responses. The third column of the form can be used for class responses that differ from the group's responses. Students sometimes find it difficult to understand that there is more than one acceptable response to or correct interpretation of literature, so they need to write other students' comments in the third column. Finally, once you feel that the students understand the terms, the third phase will consist of having students work individually on a novel and fill out the activity form by themselves. Once again, the third column can be used for comments from the class discussion. This last step creates student independence in learning.

Evaluation

The amount of credit given depends on which phase of instruction is being used. Students working independently can receive a book project grade for their novel. One suggestion is to always give credit for note taking and participating in an activity and discussion during phases one and two.

Variations

A variation of this activity is to change the second column to another story or novel for comparison and contrast. You can always vary the terms that will be covered with a particular work of literature.

ACTIVITY 3

ELEMENTS OF FICTION CHART

Definition of Term	Individual or Group Discussion	Class Discussion Responses
Title and Author		
Plot—One Sentence		
Conflict		
Protagonist— Description Antagonist— Description		
Setting		
Mood		
Irony		
Foreshadowing		
Point of View		
Theme—One Sentence		
Symbol		

ACTIVITY 4

CHARACTER COMPARISON TO SELF

Purpose of Activity

The purpose of this reading and writing activity is for students to become familiar with personality traits and descriptive language. This activity will also help students become careful readers while looking for events in the plot or behaviors to support the choice of character trait. Students will increase vocabulary through use of the words in the activity and a preliminary discussion.

How to Use the Activity

This activity can be assigned during or after reading. The vocabulary should be assigned at the onset of the activity. Each trait can be assigned a synonym and each of the character traits presented as a vocabulary map. Students need to list specific details from the novel to illustrate the chosen trait, and then must further analyze their data to decide whether they possess a similar trait. They can then discuss their decisions in class.

Evaluation

The students should be evaluated as to whether they followed directions and how much insight they gained through the activity. Students can make an oral or written summary of what they learned.

Variations

A variation of this activity would be to have the students themselves generate a list of character traits to choose from. Another would be to have the students look for classmates who have similar traits and discuss the advantages and disadvantages of having that particular trait.

ACTIVITY 4

CHARACTER COMPARISON TO SELF

Name: _____ Date: _____

Title: _____

Author: _____

Publisher and year: _____

Directions: Choose an important character. As you read your novel, look for specific traits—descriptive adjectives—that apply to the character. The traits may be stated or inferred as you read. Write down the event or behavior that displays the trait listed. Then explain whether the character trait is one that you have or that someone you know has.

CHARACTER'S NAME

Trait	Event or Behavior from the Plot	Similar or Different to Self

Some Choices of Character Traits to Consider:

These traits have positive connotations:
kind, trustworthy, friendly, honest, sincere, determined, hardworking, serious, communicative, interested, curious, humorous, candid, open-minded.

These traits have negative connotations:
rude, ignorant, rough, hardened, uneducated, illiterate, loud, quick-tempered, mean, sloppy, flighty, restless, unfocused, dirty, unorganized, irresponsible, talkative.

ACTIVITY 5

CLASS NEWSPAPER ON A NOVEL

Purpose of the Activity

There are several purposes for this activity. The first is for students to use their reading and writing skills to create a project that shows inferential understanding of a novel. Because readers must move beyond the literal text of the novel, they will practice their higher-level comprehension skills. Also, students will learn different kinds and purposes of writing. Second, students must review their understanding of the parts of a newspaper in order to complete their assignments. Third, students must cooperate with a partner as well as a group in order to complete the entire newspaper project.

How to Use the Activity

Use this activity as is or add or delete newspaper sections depending on what parts of the newspaper the students are familiar with or what sections have been taught in class. This activity should be used after all students have finished reading the book. Depending on the number of students in the class and their ability, you may want to assign the parts, have the students choose their parts, or randomly choose parts from a hat. If the class is large, students can work in pairs, or more than one newspaper can be completed on the same book. After the newspaper is completed, the students can share their conclusions.

Evaluation

An individual project can be evaluated in terms of the standards set by the teacher (which are set forth when the assignment is given). Some areas to consider are accuracy, creativity, originality, neatness, format, ability to meet a deadline, and completion of the part assigned. Before the newspaper is put together on construction paper, butcher block paper, or poster board, each individual or pair can present the assigned part to the class. During this sharing session, each person can be given a grade for sharing or a zero for not sharing. You can also choose to give the entire newspaper a grade if there are multiple groups.

Variations

If more than one novel is read in a class, the members of the group that reads a particular book can work together to create a newspaper on their book. Each group can then present their whole project to other groups. Students can look for blank space inside an actual newspaper to place their writing or project to make it look more authentic. Students can also create a mini-magazine instead of a newspaper if you prefer.

ACTIVITY 5

CLASS NEWSPAPER ON A NOVEL

Name: _____ Date: _____

Title: _____

Author: _____

Publisher and year: _____

Directions: A class newspaper will be created on the novel listed above. Each person or pair will be responsible for a particular part to help complete the class project.

Parts:

1. Editing—correcting and proofreading the newspaper and putting all the parts together.

2. Headline and news article—This article must be about an important event in the book and must contain the 5 W's: Who, What, When, Where, and Why, plus How.

3. Editorial—This essay must discuss an issue from the book, with the student writer stating his/her opinion and supporting it with facts from the book.

4. Feature article—This article should state a theme or message of the book, which should be supported with examples from the book.

5. Book review—This article should discuss the positive and negative aspects of the book and explain what kind of reader would be interested in this type of book.

6. Interview with a character—Pretend that you had a chance to interview a character. Write out some questions and answer them as if the character had answered them.

7. Advertisement—Create a one-page ad promoting the book to get others to read it.

8. Crossword puzzle—Create a crossword puzzle and answer key of vocabulary words from the novel.

9. Illustrations—Draw the main characters and write a description of each that includes physical, emotional, and personal qualities.

10. "Dear Abby" letter and response—Write a letter about a problem in the book and then write an answer in letter format that helps the character solve the problem.

11. Comic strip—Create a comic containing an insight or theme from the book.

12. Obituary—If there is a death in the book, write a death notice for the deceased.

ACTIVITY 6

"DEAR DIARY"

Purpose of the Activity

This activity concentrates on higher-level reading and on diary writing. Because a diary is a vehicle for response writing, students will learn about putting feelings, reactions, and insights on paper, and they have an opportunity to do so from a fictitious point of view. A lesson in point of view might be necessary to help students understand that response writing can vary greatly depending on the person doing the reacting. Finally, students will practice using facts and details from the novel to explain the character's reactions in the diary entries.

How to Use the Activity

Students can be given time in class to read and record notes for their diary entries. Another possibility is to allow students to read their novel independently and to use this activity as a post-reading writing assignment. You can decide how many entries will be sufficient for the diary sample. This activity can also be used as a choice of several projects offered to students reading the same novel or a variety of reading materials.

Evaluation

As this activity is basically a writing assignment, the teacher can stress that all entries be mechanically correct. This activity can be graded as other writing assignments would be graded. If the element of creativity is required, a portion of the evaluation can be for creativity and originality.

Variations

One possibility for creativity and variety among the diaries is to allow students to personalize the diary in terms of the character in the novel. The choice of paper (color and size), ink, illustrations, and informality of language can all be suggested or required at your discretion. The more choices the students have, the more opportunities they have to display their creativity and understanding of a character.

ACTIVITY 6

"DEAR DIARY"

Name: _____ Date: _____

Title: _____

Author: _____

Publisher and year: _____

Directions: As you read your novel or after you finish it, take on the identity of one of the characters and write entries in an imaginary diary. Each entry should be at least a paragraph in length. The entries should be written from the point of view of the character and dated (even if you have to make up a date). The entries need not be for successive days, as they represent part of a complete diary maintained by the character to record the events and his or her reactions as revealed in the novel. The entries should reflect personal reactions to the character's involvement with one of the following:

- major plot episodes

- relationships with other characters

- positive or negative feelings

- insights gained through experience

- observations of the setting (place, time, and culture)

You will have to use inference skills to piece together the facts in order to make educated guesses about the character's thoughts and feelings based on the information given by the author. The sample below can be used as a guide to note taking while reading and to remember specific details for support and accuracy later when the entries are being written.

Outline of Entries:

	Pages from Novel	Section from Novel	Date	Reaction
1.				
2.				
3.				
4.				
5.				

ACTIVITY 7

STORY MAP

Purpose of the Activity

The purpose of this activity is for students to show their understanding of a novel. Because all short stories and novels contain the same basic elements of fiction, using the elements of fiction repeatedly in a graphic organizer helps the students see the similarities among all stories. The story map provides students a way of keeping track of important information from the story as they read or after they have finished a book.

How to Use the Activity

Define the terms and model the use of the story map before students complete the form on their own. A children's book or short story can be used before the activity is used on a novel. If students are familiar with the terms, they can work individually, in pairs, or in groups. This activity is also helpful for class discussions.

Evaluation

You may choose to evaluate this activity as a class assignment or as homework. The amount of credit for this activity will depend on its purpose. The items to consider are completeness, accuracy, and following your guidelines.

Variations

You can make changes in the form if more information is desired. Another suggestion is for students to practice summary writing. On the back of the activity sheet, you can have the students write either a one-sentence or one-paragraph summary of the novel. Summary writing is sometimes difficult for students because they need to include the beginning, middle, and end of a story in a particular format. This activity can be made into a template on the computer so that students can fill it in and gain word processing practice as well.

ACTIVITY 7

STORY MAP

Name: _____Date: _____

Title: _____

Author: _____

Publisher and year: _____

SETTING

Where: _____ When: _____

CHARACTERS

Protagonist: _____

Description (3 Qualities): 1. _____

2._____ 3. _____

Antagonist: _____

Description (3 Qualities): 1. _____

2._____ 3. _____

CONFLICT

Problem 1. _____ 2. _____

PLOT EVENTS OF STORY

Event 1: _____

Event 2: _____

Event 3: _____

Event 4: _____

Event 5: _____

READER'S FEELINGS OR MOOD

Feeling: _____ Happening in Book: _____

Feeling: _____ Happening in Book: _____

ONE-SENTENCE THEME

_____

_____

ACTIVITY 8

LETTER TO A FRIEND ABOUT A NOVEL

Purpose of the Activity

The purpose of this activity is to provide a vehicle for students to communicate to other students about a book that they are reading or have just read. The inclusion of questions within the framework of the letter allows students to answer the letter if you want to pursue the communication further. In addition, the students learn the format of a friendly letter.

How to Use the Activity

Depending on the ability of the students, you can use this form as a frame for students to follow specifically, or you may want to use it as an example for students, loosely adding, changing, or deleting the requested information. Letter writing between students can be done within a class or outside of class. The writing can be done in class or in a computer lab, where students can change seats and read the letter on the computer. Also, students will become more familiar with other books through the letter exchange.

Evaluation

This writing activity can be used as a post-reading book report, or it can be used during writing assignments. Communication among students can take place while students read their novels so that more questions can be asked. Readers would be able to answer the questions as more of the novel is read.

Variations

After students become familiar with letter writing and understand the novel because of discussion and other classwork, you may want the class to brainstorm other topics and questions that can be included in a letter about the book. This activity is particularly interesting if students in the class read a variety of books, or several novels are read by various groups. This project can also be used in conjunction with teaching the business letter. A comparison and contrast discussion can help students understand the format differences of and the purposes for each type of letter.

ACTIVITY 8

LETTER TO A FRIEND ABOUT A NOVEL

Name: _____Date: _____

Title: _____

Author: _____

Publisher and year: _____

Directions: You are to write a letter to a friend in the class about your novel. You can use this form as a rough draft to include important information about the book.

Date_____

Dear _____,

    I am reading (or I have just finished reading) a novel called _____, by _____, the author. It was about a character named _____, who has a problem (state the conflict). The story is about (state the plot in two or three sentences). The main character is similar to me because (explain ways and reasons). However, the character is different from me because (explain ways and reasons). When I consider all his/her characteristics, I think the character is very similar/very different from me (choose one).

    I like (or dislike) this book for three reasons: (explain the reasons with support from the book in this paragraph).

    This would be a really great book for someone to read if they like _____ kinds of books. It contains _____ and _____ that readers would enjoy. The next book that I would like to read would be a _____ kind of book. Write back soon about the book you are reading (or have just finished). Let me know about: (ask three questions that you would like answered in your friend's response.) Talk to you soon. Bye.

Sincerely,

(sign your name here)

Type your name

ACTIVITY 9

"WHAT IF?" SITUATIONS FOR THE PROTAGONIST

Purpose of the Activity

The purpose of this reading/writing activity is to have students write, use inferences, and support their ideas. Students must make educated guesses about the main character's choices based on the knowledge that they glean from reading the book and understanding the character. Although there is no single correct response to any of the questions, the students must provide specific examples from the novel to convince the audience of their choices.

How to Use the Activity

You can use these suggestions for topics or provide others for students to choose from. This activity can be used as a writing assignment in class, for homework, or for a test. The students can share their essays with other members of the class, so that this writing activity can be used as a springboard for discussion and debate.

Evaluation

This activity can be graded as any other writing assignment would be graded. You can determine how many sentences, details, or paragraphs are required. Rather than you grading the essay alone, students can be involved in the process by looking for details that prove their classmates' contentions.

Variations

Students often enjoy the creativity of this unusual essay format. An interesting variation on this theme asks questions about people who are making a movie based on the novel. Students can decide who would play the female lead, male lead, and antagonist.

ACTIVITY 9

"WHAT IF?" SITUATIONS FOR THE PROTAGONIST

Name: _____ Date: _____

Title: _____

Author: _____

Publisher and year: _____

Directions: Choose one of the suggested situations for your main character and write an essay completing the topic sentence with one of the choices. Make sure that your choice is supported with specific details from the book, because you are making an inference that should be based on facts.

1. The main character, _____, will probably die:
   a) in a car accident
   b) of a strange disease
   c) of a broken heart
   d) by lethal injection
   e) choose another method _____

2. If the main character, _____, could choose a vacation place, he/she would prefer:
   a) sunbathing in Hawaii
   b) camping in the Rocky Mountains
   c) fishing in Wisconsin
   d) skiing in Europe
   e) choose another destination _____

3. For his birthday, the main character, _____, would like the following gift:
   a) a motorcycle
   b) a $200 gift certificate to a clothing store
   c) a computer
   d) a case of beer
   e) choose another gift _____

4. The main character, _____, wins the One Million Dollar Lottery and must decide what to do with the money. His/Her choice is to:
   a) give some or all of it to charity
   b) take a trip around the world
   c) go into hiding in the mountains
   d) buy lots of materialistic things
   e) choose another spending choice _____

From *What a Novel Idea!* © 1997 Katherine Wiesolek Kuta. Teacher Ideas Press. 1-800-237-6124.

ACTIVITY 10

MATCHING SYMBOLS WITH CHARACTERS

Purpose of the Activity

The purpose of this reading/writing activity is for students to make inferences and think at a higher level. Students need to understand a character's personality, traits, and behavioral motivation in order to choose an appropriate symbol or logo to represent that character. Additionally, the students need to explain why they chose the symbol using specific reasons. This activity involves students in reading carefully for details as well as referring back to the novel to look for descriptions or behaviors to support the choice of symbol.

How to Use the Activity

In order for this activity to make sense to students, some preliminary work may need to be done. You may want to discuss the role of symbols and logos in society and their various uses. Some examples from advertising, business cards, objects, or stationery can be brought into the classroom as models and for discussion. A class assignment might be to ask students to look for examples in their everyday world. You can use this activity during reading if you want the students to read for the purpose of character understanding and specific support. The activity can also be used after reading in pairs, groups, or individually so that students need to analyze the character's complete development from the beginning to the end of the novel. Students can share their responses with others and compare and contrast their choices as well as the reasons for their choices. A discussion can follow on flat versus round characters and static versus dynamic characters. It is important for students to realize that in everyday life, people make judgments about others all the time.

Evaluation

You should give credit to students who complete the assignment and give logical reasons for their choices. There may or may not be a specific symbol match for each character being discussed. Encourage open discussion and be willing to accept diverse choices of the students if these choices are supported with details from the novel.

Variations

This activity is in no way limited to the symbols that are printed. You can supply the students with numerous other choices. You can also ask students to look through magazines or newspapers for better symbols or logos for characters. Another possibility is for students to draw their own logos or symbols. It is also interesting to ask students to draw logos or symbols that would best represent themselves. This would provide insight into the students and their perceptions about themselves.

ACTIVITY 10

MATCHING SYMBOLS WITH CHARACTERS

Name: _____ Date: _____

Title: _____

Author: _____

Publisher and year: _____

Directions: Write the names of three characters from the novel below. Then choose a symbol or logo that would be appropriate for the character based on the information given in the book. In the space provided, explain why the symbol matches each character's personality.

CHARACTER'S NAME   **SYMBOL**   **REASON**

1.

2.

3.

Symbols (Choose one or draw your own):

ACTIVITY 11

WRITING A NEWSPAPER ARTICLE

Purpose of the Activity

There are several purposes for this reading/writing activity as the students are asked to use their reading, judgment, and writing skills to accomplish this task. First, the students will read a novel and complete an activity using details from the book. Second, the students will improve their reading because they will learn to read for a specific purpose as well as to relate fictional material to real-world possibilities. Third, the students will write a newspaper article in a particular format in order to learn about journalistic writing. Last, students will display their understanding of the novel while being creative.

How to Use the Activity

This activity can be assigned during reading so that the students can read carefully and document meaningful events from the book that would make good front-page stories. If you assign this activity after the students have finished reading the novel, they can go back to the novel and make judgments about the incidents in order to choose one to write about for the news story. To increase background knowledge, review the form of a news story and have the students read samples in the classroom.

Evaluation

The students' projects should be evaluated in terms of whether the project followed the assignment's directions. Another consideration is the quality of the newspaper story and its accuracy in following details from the novel. A third consideration is the creativity of the layout, photo inclusion, and headlines, and possibly the sharing of the story with the class as well. Students can be involved in the evaluation of the project by looking for accuracy, deciding which are the best news stories, and explaining their reasons for their choices.

Variations

Students can look in a newspaper for blank spaces to cut out and save so that the articles can be pasted onto them and made to look like a real newspaper. Students can also type their news stories right on the blank newspaper. Depending on how much of the newspaper and its parts that you want to teach, you can also ask part of the class to write a feature story based on a human-interest topic discussed in the novel. Then you and the class can discuss the news and feature stories and why their placement is so important.

ACTIVITY 11

WRITING A NEWSPAPER ARTICLE

Name: _____ Date: _____

Title: _____

Author: _____

Publisher and year: _____

1. Select three important events from your novel that involve action, adventure, or a turning point. Also write the chapter or page number for reference later.

_____

_____

_____

2. Narrow down your selection of a topic for an interesting news story by asking someone which would be an interesting topic.

Name of person and his/her choice: _____

3. Select one event and write a news story that would make the front page of the newspaper if the event were true. All news stories include the five W's: who, what, where, when, and why, plus how.

Incident from Novel and Page Number for Story

WHO_____ WHAT _____

WHEN_____ WHERE _____

WHY_____ HOW _____

4. Think of a catchy headline to use as a title for the news story.

_____

5. You may want to supply a picture, photo, or illustration to be included in the story.

ACTIVITY 12

STUDENT-CREATED TEST

Purpose of the Activity

There are several purposes for this reading/writing activity. The students must follow a format to write a test on their novel to get experience in writing tests. They will focus on the main points and details that they feel are important enough to get tested on. Second, the students must take the test to provide an answer key that will display both knowledge about the novel and their writing skills.

How to Use the Activity

This activity can be used immediately after reading a novel or as an alternate type of book report. The class can read a single novel, or individuals can choose their own books. You can choose questions from the students' tests to make up a test for the class. Students can also take each other's tests if the quality of the tests meets your standards.

Evaluation

The students' test projects can be graded as any book report would be evaluated. Some factors to consider are the ability of the student to follow the directions of the format, the focus of the questions on the content, and the accuracy of the answer key in terms of the facts, details, and inferences made from the novel.

Variations

A variation of this activity is to change the format of the test or even eliminate it. One way to do this and add more student involvement is to ask the students to brainstorm the different kinds of tests that they like and find effective. Of course, you can add to or subtract from the information asked for in the activity.

ACTIVITY 12

STUDENT-CREATED TEST

Name: _____ Date: _____

Title: _____

Author: _____

Publisher and year: _____

Directions: You are to write and create a test based on the format listed below. Then you are to take the test and supply an answer key.

Part 1. Write five multiple-choice questions about the plot, covering the major events of the story. These questions can include conflict, exposition, rising action, climax, falling action, or resolution.

Part 2. Write five questions that can be matched with choices. These questions should be about the characters in the story and traits that are identifiable.

Part 3. Write five fill-in-the-blank questions. These will be short-answer blanks. Topics to include might be foreshadowing, symbolism, irony, setting, mood, or point of view.

Part 4. Write five sentences with blanks for vocabulary so the test taker can figure out the meaning of the word by how it is used in context in the sentence. Make sure to include a list of several words to choose from.

Part 5. Write two essay questions that require a one-paragraph response from the test taker. Possible topics include the theme or message of the book, the suggested audience for the book, the reader's liking or disliking of the book, and a controversial issue in the book.

Part 6. Evaluate the difficulty in writing a test.

_____

_____

_____

_____

_____

ACTIVITY 13

LETTER FROM ONE CHARACTER TO ANOTHER

Purpose of the Activity

Although this activity is primarily a writing activity, the students must have done some reading of the novel or have completed it to understand the characters enough to think and write as they would. Also, depending on the choice of topics, the students will discuss their understanding of the issues or elements of the story. Finally, the students will learn the parts of a friendly letter and practice this form of communication.

How to Use the Activity

This activity can be used during or after reading. The students will probably have the greatest understanding of the characters at the conclusion of the reading. However, if you want the students to make predictions, discuss a problem, or help in the decision process, then this activity would be useful during the reading of the book. It might be useful for students to share their letters with a partner or the entire class. This would allow them to discuss each other's feelings as well as to critique and question what others think and have written.

Evaluation

The students' written project should be evaluated as any piece of writing would be assessed. Another possibility for evaluation is for the students to discuss the topic in the letter and the accuracy and insight of the writer into the character. The assessment can be done in the form of a simple rubric, with the standards made clear to all students. The class can vote for the best letters, and those letters can be answered.

Variations

In addition to writing to a character in the book, the letters can be randomly passed out to students so they can be answered as an in-class writing assignment. The letters can then be returned to the authors to read the responses. Students like to correspond with one another, and this activity would allow them to do so as they take on the personalities and points of view of the characters from the novel. Because the second paragraph consists of questions asked by the writer, a response that answered those questions would not be out of order.

ACTIVITY 13

LETTER FROM ONE CHARACTER TO ANOTHER

Name: _____ Date: _____

Title: _____

Author: _____

Publisher and year: _____

Directions: You are to write a friendly letter from one character to another character in the novel and discuss one or more of the following topics. Then have the other character answer the letter.

1. Describe a problem and ask for solutions in resolving a conflict. Make sure to stay in character and write what the character would write.

2. Discuss an issue of importance, such as violence, drugs, or parents, and explain the character's feelings on the subject.

3. Imagine you are contacting a character after the end of the novel, and you want to predict what has happened to the character and ask questions about another character's life.

4. Explain an incident from the book where an event dramatically changed that character's life and taught him/her something. The letter could be directed to a character from another book or story where there was a similar change in character.

5. Relate several incidents, clues, and foreshadowing that a character used to help solve a problem, mystery, or adventure. The character could be writing the letter to a minor character or character you make up who was unable to follow the case.

                                                    Date

Dear (Name of character),

        (indent) Make it clear which of the above topics you are writing about by giving a short explanation of the plot.

        (2d paragraph) You may want to ask questions that you want the person to whom you are writing to answer.

                                                    Sincerely,

                                    (sign your name and type it below your signature)

ACTIVITY 14

FORMAL LETTER TO AN AUTHOR

Purpose of the Activity

There are several purposes for this writing/reading activity. First, the students must read a novel carefully and critically, with the purpose of corresponding with the writer and offering their opinions of the work. Second, the students must learn the business letter format in order to complete the writing assignment. Third, the students are writing to a real person, who hopefully will answer their letters and involve them in real-life communication. Fourth, the students can research information about the author and her/his background so they can ask intelligent questions.

How to Use the Activity

This activity can be used when students read novels of their own choosing. Each student writes to a different person so that the class learns about a variety of authors. When the students start reading, you may want to tell them that they will be writing to the authors of their novels, so they should take notes on likes and dislikes as they read. The notes will provide students with specific information to include in the letter. You can provide the students with addresses for the authors, or you can have the students do this research themselves. One possibility is for students to write to authors in care of the publishers of their books. The form for this activity should be used as a guide or rough draft for students to give them ideas and show them the business letter format.

Evaluation

This activity should consist of an initial rough draft of the letter, a final draft to be graded, and a corrected perfect copy to be sent to the author. A grade can also be given for addressing an envelope correctly and enclosing the folded letter.

Variations

Students can use the school's address or their home addresses on the envelope for replies. If home addresses are used, the students can bring in the replies to share with the class for extra credit. Make a copy of the replies for a file for future reference.

ACTIVITY 14

FORMAL LETTER TO AN AUTHOR

Name: _____ Date: _____

Title: _____

Author: _____

Publisher and year: _____

        Your address _____

        Your city, state, ZIP code _____

        Date _____

Name of author_____

Address of author_____

City, state, ZIP code of author_____

Dear Mr. or Ms. _____:

Explain your reason for writing the letter. _____.

Give information about you and your school. _____

_____.

Tell what you liked about the book and/or a particular part, character, or section of the book and why. _____

_____

Ask a question or two about something that you do not understand in the book. You could ask about future writing or a sequel._____

_____

_____

Sincerely,

Allow space for your signature and type your name underneath it.

ACTIVITY 15

WRITING AN ADDITIONAL CHAPTER FOR A NOVEL

Purpose of the Activity

The main purpose of this activity is for students to think and write creatively by adding a chapter to the novel that they have just finished reading. The students must make inferences about the characters' future and behavior that are consistent with what the characters have said and done in the novel.

How to Use the Activity

Assign one or all of the choices listed for additional chapters. You can brainstorm with the class on one of the choices and have the students discuss the positive and negative points of having the novel continue in such a manner. (A full-page brainstorming sheet is included on page 137.) The students can also work in groups as they prewrite, outline, draft, revise, edit, and proofread. Another suggestion is to allow students to share their writing with other individuals, groups, or the entire class. Reading an individual's or group's work to an audience helps instill pride in the piece of writing.

Evaluation

Evaluate the additional chapter to the novel as a writing assignment and grade it according to the conditions set forth for the class. Some factors to consider are the writing process, group cooperation, meeting length requirements, and content. Each chapter's content can be discussed and voted on by the class members, noting such elements as accuracy, characterization, plot continuity, and resolution of the story. Sharing writing with class members can also be part of the entire grade.

Variations

A variation for the use of this activity is to offer it as one of several choices for students to choose from for the book project. Any group of activities from this book can be combined for students to choose from. Letting students make their own choices gives them a feeling of power over their decisions and their work, and sometimes students are more motivated to finish their tasks if they have some control over their choices.

ACTIVITY 15

WRITING AN ADDITIONAL CHAPTER FOR A NOVEL

Name: _____ Date: _____

Title: _____

Author: _____

Publisher and year: _____

Directions: After you finish the novel, write an additional chapter for the novel. You must make predictions and educated guesses (inferences) based on the facts and details in the book. Listed below are some possibilities to think about.

1. Write about a career choice, relationship, or lifestyle choice for a main character either immediately after the end of the book or five years in the future.

2. Write about how another problem in the book was handled by a minor character who may not have been used sufficiently by the author.

3. Write about a new situation that a character becomes involved in so that this new plotline would be a setup for a possible sequel.

4. Write about the next day or the next week of a character's life that would expand upon the resolution of the story.

5. Many times an author ends a story without wrapping up all the loose ends. Think of several questions that remain unanswered at the conclusion of the book. Choose one and decide how it should be answered in your additional chapter.

Brainstorm and write some possibilities for additional chapters here:

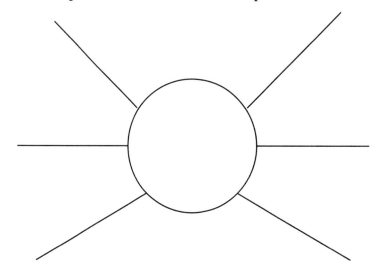

ACTIVITY 16

WRITING A NEW ENDING

Purpose of the Activity

This post-reading/writing project has two purposes. First, because the students must finish reading before they are able to complete this activity and rewrite the ending, this activity involves inference skills and application skills. Students must understand the characters and the plot in order to replace the author's ending. The plot sequence must make sense and be logical according to the preceding action. Second, the students will practice their creative writing skills by actually being authors. Also, they must justify their reasons for changing the ending to the new ending that they rewrite.

How to Use the Activity

This activity should be assigned after the students have finished reading the novel. The suggestions on the activity sheet are to help point the students toward directions to pursue in their writing. You can assign particular suggestions to individuals or groups if the entire class is reading the same novel. Another possibility is to allow students to choose the directions that they wish the new ending to follow. Pairing students to listen to each other's rough drafts will enable peer editors to check for whether the new ending makes sense, is logical, and accurately uses facts and details from the book.

Evaluation

The students' assessment can include the writing process as well as the final product. The writing process should include the steps of prewriting, drafting, editing, and revising until a final draft is turned in as a new chapter. You might have the new endings read aloud to the whole class, and the class can choose the best new ending. This would give the students practice in their reading, listening, and speaking skills.

Variations

One variation for this activity is for students to think beyond the idea of a new ending and create a new character who can be introduced during the book or at the new ending. Students can write a new story that features new characters.

Another possibility is to have the students create an ending that would allow the author to write a sequel. The students can also write a new first chapter for a new book and begin where the original novel ends the plot. The students can also imagine what the story would have been like if the setting had been changed or a character had been eliminated. You can also ask the students to suggest story variations.

ACTIVITY 16

WRITING A NEW ENDING

Name: _____ Date: _____

Title: _____

Author: _____

Publisher and year: _____

Directions: After finishing the novel, write a new ending for the book. You have the opportunity to be creative and change the resolution (ending) of the story. The restrictions are that you must stay in the point of view of the author, and the characters must retain their character traits. The new ending must make sense and be believable.

Here are some suggestions for ideas that may or may not apply to your book:

1. The problem could be resolved differently than the author resolved it.

2. The main characters learn (or do not learn) from their experiences.

3. The ending can be changed from happy to tragic.

4. Changing the decision of a particular character could change what happens to other people.

5. Irony could be introduced in the story with a strange or unexpected turn of events.

6. New information about a protagonist or antagonist that you reveal can help create a new ending.

7. New evidence or facts can be disclosed that solve a mystery or suspense story in a different way.

8. The story can end in an open-ended way that makes the reader want some questions answered (possibly in a sequel).

9. The focus of the ending can be on a symbol of importance that may not have been obvious earlier in the novel.

Of course, you can come up with an idea of your own.

ACTIVITY 17

CHOOSING A CHARACTER AS A FRIEND

Purpose of the Activity

There are several purposes for this during or after reading/writing activity. First, it involves expository writing that gives the students practice in supporting one's opinions with facts and details from a text. It also teaches the students paragraph format and the use of transitions in writing. Finally, the students will make critical judgments, which are necessary in life, especially when choosing friends. The values that the students find important will become apparent by the character they choose to have as a friend, which will open up discussion in the classroom.

How to Use the Activity

While the students are reading their novel, tell them the topic of the writing assignment so they can take notes and look for information while they read. Another approach to the activity is for students to be given the topic as a post-reading activity in which they must go back into the novel to look for support for their contentions. With this approach, the students must do more analysis afterward and become familiar enough with the text to locate specific information. You can choose which approach is better for your students based on their abilities and your goals.

Evaluation

The writing project can be graded like any other writing assignment. Some factors to consider are content, writing skills, and ability to follow directions. The students' ability to meet a deadline is also another consideration.

Variations

A variation for this writing assignment is to assign the topic for a theme of several paragraphs in length. The assignment can also be given as one of several writing topics from which the students can make their selections. Also, the students can share their writing assignments with other members of the class and discuss their choices. The activity form can be used as a rough or final draft.

ACTIVITY 17

CHOOSING A CHARACTER AS A FRIEND

Name: _____ Date: _____

Title: _____

Author: _____

Publisher and year: _____

Directions: Write a paragraph of at least _____sentences in which you explain the reasons for choosing a particular character from your novel that you would like to have as a friend. Give specific characteristics and incidents from the book that led you to your decision.

Name of character:_____

Title

Topic sentence: It would be exciting or fun or special or _____ (choose

one word) to be a friend of _____, from the novel _____

_____, by _____,

for many reasons. First, _____

_____

Second, _____

_____

Third, _____

_____

Fourth, _____

_____

Therefore, _____

_____

ACTIVITY 18

SUMMARY OF A BOOK WITHIN A SYMBOL OR LOGO

Purpose of the Activity

There are several purposes for this post-reading/writing activity. First, it requires higher-level thinking and evaluating skills as well as some creativity in order to complete the task. The students are asked to rate the book similarly to a movie rating system, using stars to show their opinion of the novel's worth. Second, they must be creative to draw a symbol to represent the book. Third, they condense many ideas into a small number of words.

How to Use the Activity

Students can use the following page as a prepared form or they can use a computer or paper and markers to design a symbol to represent the book. Then they should write, type, or cut and paste the information to fit into the object. The symbol should be large enough to contain several sentences in one form or another. By having the students write inside this small space, it limits the amount of writing they can do and forces them to carefully choose their words for specific meaning. You may want the students to share their projects with other students.

Evaluation

This book project can be evaluated as any written assignment would be assessed. Besides the accuracy of the information, consider whether the students met the requirements of the assignment by completing the written information on the activity sheet. The creative element is always difficult to assess, but as long as the students have good reasons for choosing symbols that they consider appropriate for their novels, the objects are acceptable.

Variations

The students can display their objects on a bulletin board or in some other fashion. If the class is reading a variety of books, have the students guess which object and its information match which novel. Finally, the quotes can be used as reader responses later in the course.

ACTIVITY 18

SUMMARY OF A BOOK WITHIN A SYMBOL OR LOGO

Name: _____ Date: _____

Title: _____

Author: _____

Publisher and year: _____

Rating (one to five stars): _____

Directions: Think of a symbol, logo, or object that can represent the entire book in some way. Draw it large enough to include the following information:

- THREE- TO FIVE-SENTENCE SUMMARY that includes major characters and the plot sequence

- A PHRASE OR SENTENCE WORTH QUOTING

- ONE SENTENCE STATING WHAT YOU LIKED OR DISLIKED ABOUT THE STORY

ACTIVITY 19

VOCABULARY EXCHANGE:
REPLACING WORDS IN PASSAGES WITH SYNONYMS

Purpose of the Activity

The purpose of this activity involves vocabulary and contextual meanings of words. First, the readers must consider the type of word to underline and its part of speech in order to successfully replace it with two other words of the same type and meaning. Next, have the students peer share and evaluate each others' choices. Finally, students practice working with the thesaurus and see how important word choices become for a writer.

How to Use the Activity

This activity can be used with a novel during or after reading. You can choose the page and passage or allow the students to choose. This activity can be assigned in addition to another book project on a novel. Students may or may not be allowed to use dictionaries or thesauruses, depending on the vocabulary of class members. Sometimes students need to learn to consider word choices in order to convey the most precise meaning of their thoughts. You can use a passage from a novel as a model for students to understand how to proceed on their own. You can also have students work in pairs or groups to discuss word choices.

Evaluation

This activity can be assessed as a class activity or as a homework assignment. Remember that changing a particular word can sometimes change the meaning of a sentence or passage. Students should become aware of this as they discuss each other's word choices.

Variations

To teach a little more grammar, have the students label the part of speech of the words that they underlined in the passage. The students could help each other understand how words are used in sentences. Students can also look for sentence variety and label simple, compound, and complex sentences. You can extend this exercise even further by having students do some or all of the above on their own compositions in the future.

ACTIVITY 19

VOCABULARY EXCHANGE:
REPLACING WORDS IN PASSAGES WITH SYNONYMS

Name: _____ Date: _____

Title: _____

Author: _____

Publisher and year: _____

Directions: Select part of a page from your book and write it exactly as it appears in the book. Make sure you complete the line, paragraph, and passage. Underline at least 10 words. Then find two synonyms that can replace each underlined word. Write the synonyms directly above the word.

Page number in novel: _____

_____

_____

_____

_____

_____

_____

_____

_____

Now ask a peer to read the passage and comment on the meaning of or information in the passage. Does your peer think the meaning changes with the substitutions of the vocabulary? How?

ACTIVITY 20

PLOT SEQUENCE AND RESPONSE WRITING

Purpose of the Activity

There are several purposes for this activity. The main one is to actively involve the students in the reading process by reading for a purpose. By having the students write a summary of what was just read, they must think about the material, comprehend the action, condense the ideas into a concise statement, and put their thoughts on paper in one sentence. The response writing involves the students by having them interact with the text in the form of a prediction, question, reaction, or opinion.

How to Use the Activity

This during-reading activity should be used by the students each time they read the novel. Allow class time for the reading and writing during sustained silent reading for the first 10 minutes of class. The students can also log entries during other sittings of novel reading. The activity can be collected on the date the students finish reading the novel. If all the students are reading the same novel, they can read one chapter a day and log one entry on this form. The form can be duplicated for additional chapters as needed.

Evaluation

Grade the participation of the students not only in reading the novel but also in making the entries for each chapter. You can use this activity as a project in itself or as background preliminary information for a larger assignment, such as one on all the elements of fiction or another project from this book.

Variations

Change the idea of logging chapters to logging each time the students read, whether the chapter is completed or not. An advantage of following this format is to have students accountable for every class and home reading if a certain number of entries are required. This form can also be used for oral readings done in class. The students work on listening skills while they listen for a specific purpose, and must write a summary and a response.

ACTIVITY 20

PLOT SEQUENCE AND RESPONSE WRITING

Name: _____ Date: _____

Title: _____

Author: _____

Publisher and year: _____

Directions: As you read your novel, write a one-sentence summary and a response statement for each chapter on this form. Make sure to include the date for each entry. This activity is due when you finish reading the book.

Plot Summary:
- actual events from the book

Response:
- a prediction of what will happen next
- a question about something you don't understand
- a reaction to something a character did or said
- an opinion about what you liked, disliked, or found interesting

Chapter Date Summary Sentence and Response Sentence

Chapter	Date	Summary Sentence and Response Sentence
1.		**PLOT** **RESPONSE**
2.		**PLOT** **RESPONSE**
3.		**PLOT** **RESPONSE**

Chapter Date   Summary Sentence and Response Sentence

Chapter	Date	Summary Sentence and Response Sentence
4.		**PLOT** **RESPONSE**
5.		**PLOT** **RESPONSE**
6.		**PLOT** **RESPONSE**
7.		**PLOT** **RESPONSE**
8.		**PLOT** **RESPONSE**
9.		**PLOT** **RESPONSE**
10.		**PLOT** **RESPONSE**

Representing and Viewing
Standards Activities

ACTIVITY 21

POSTER ADVERTISEMENT FOR THE NOVEL

Purpose of the Activity

This activity is a post-reading one because the students must use higher-level thinking skills and process beyond the literal level to draw inferences about the characters, symbols, and theme of the novel. They must also write a short persuasive review. The main purpose of the representing/viewing activity is for the students to design posters for their novels that promote the reading of the book by others, in particular their classmates or other teenagers. The poster is also a representation of the students' knowledge and understanding of the novel. A book review is included as part of the activity so that the students can make solid judgments and learn to support their beliefs. Drawings and pictures allow for creativity and variation and also teach students about the placement of graphics and information on a poster. This activity easily sets up the process of presenting the poster to the class for further learning about a book.

How to Use the Activity

This activity can be assigned after a class novel or individual novels have been read. If the class is reading a variety of books, oral presentations of the posters allow the students to become familiar with many titles for future reading. Depending on the ability of the class, you can have the students work in the class on the project, or it can be an assignment done on their own. Students can be given some flexibility to add or change the information requested. The size of the poster should be decided by the teacher (two feet by two feet is large enough so that all class members can see it during a presentation). Butcher block paper, poster board, or art paper works well. Before you start, ask students to look at movie posters, billboards, or other advertisements and make observations in a journal for a discussion about placement and other details for a catchy appearance.

Evaluation

The poster project can be graded on a variety of factors such as accuracy, attractiveness, completeness of information, insights, meeting a deadline, and creativity. Students should be given the criteria at the onset of the project. Sharing of the project can also be a grade. Sometimes, to relieve anxiety, a simple "A" or "0" can be given for the experience of presenting orally. You can decide on the weight of the grade.

Variations

Ask students to brainstorm what information should be placed on a poster, and give the students more flexibility in the actual design of the project. Once again, this activity can be used as one of several choices for book projects.

ACTIVITY 21

POSTER ADVERTISEMENT FOR THE NOVEL

Name: _____ Date: _____

Title: _____

Author: _____

Publisher and year: _____

Directions: Your assignment is to design a poster to promote the reading of your book by your classmates as well as others. It is also a means of sharing your reading experiences with your peers. The model below is a possible format for the poster. You should try to show creativity, be original, and display understanding of the novel.

QUOTATION FROM BOOK
EXPLAIN SIGNIFICANCE AND MEANING

QUOTATION FROM BOOK
SIGNIFICANCE AND MEANING

PICTURES OF CHARACTERS
AND DESCRIPTIVE ADJECTIVES

SYMBOLS OF IMPORTANCE
AND THEIR MEANING

CATCHY EXPRESSION
SUCH AS "I LIKED IT! YOU WILL TOO! READ!!!"

TITLE

AUTHOR

PUBLISHER AND YEAR

POSSIBLY DRAWINGS OR PICTURES ON THE TOPIC

ONE-SENTENCE THEME

SHORT REVIEW OF WHY OTHERS
SHOULD READ THE BOOK

ACTIVITY 22

THEMATIC COLLAGE

Purpose of the Activity

This activity not only involves reading and some writing, but it also emphasizes the standards of representing and viewing. The students are given the opportunity to represent the novel's ideas in the form of a collage, a careful placement of a variety of pictures to display an appropriate theme or motif from the book. This hands-on activity allows students to be creative and original with their ideas as well as to think symbolically. This activity can easily be shared with others through a presentation and explanation of the pictorial representation. When students do formal booktalks on their novels and collages, they share their knowledge and insights about the novel with others. They also practice their speaking skills in front of an audience, and the class members learn how to act appropriately as an audience.

How to Use the Activity

This activity can be used after a book (a class novel or individual book) has been finished. If an entire class has read the same novel, class members can sign up for different themes, motifs, or topics present in the work. The choices listed on the worksheet are popular themes and motifs that apply to many novels. The expectations of the presentation are suggestions for a one-minute booktalk on the collage.

Evaluation

For assessment, you can evaluate the quality of the collage as well as the accuracy of and explanation for the pictorial display. At the beginning of the reading, the students should know what the criteria are for the assessment. The presentation and the expectations for the audience should be discussed with the students. The presentation can be counted as a speech and graded as any normal speech, or it can be counted as a sharing experience where students would receive a grade of credit or no credit.

Variations

The class members can brainstorm the themes and motifs for the collages. Also, students can work in pairs or groups. Allow slower students to use class time to work on the project. Ask students to bring in old magazines, newspapers, and catalogs to cut up in the classroom. These can be kept for future projects.

ACTIVITY 22

THEMATIC COLLAGE

Name: _____ Date: _____

Title: _____

Author: _____

Publisher and year: _____

Choose one of the themes or motifs below that seems appropriate for your novel. Then portray this theme with a careful selection of pictures, words, and images. Be ready to explain to your peers the significance of all your selections.

Possible Choices:
1. Appearances vs. reality
2. Responsibility means learning that there are consequences for one's actions
3. Learning leads to self-discovery
4. Trust is earned
5. Friendship
6. The value of time
7. One does not appreciate something until it is gone
8. Love is mysterious and complicated
9. Decisions are based on values
10. Reading for pleasure should be a lifelong habit

Collage Presentation:
A presentation is expected the day the project is due. You will share the following:
1. Name the title, author, and publisher, and show the book.
2. Show the collage.
3. Relate the theme or motif to the novel and other students.
4. Explain the significance of the graphics chosen.
5. Say whether you liked the book or not and why.

Suggestions:
1. The collage should be large enough for all members of the class to see.
2. Use old magazines, old newspapers, and old photographs.
3. Practice arranging the items before you actually glue.

ACTIVITY 23

BOOKMARK

Purpose of Activity

There are several purposes for this reading, writing, representing, and viewing activity. The students must first read the novel and then write and be creative concisely. They must create a different kind of format for displaying their analysis and interpretation of a work of literature. The bookmark format allows the students to be creative and original, but by giving them a specific format, you are requiring some higher-level thinking skills and critical analysis to be done in a concise space. Another purpose of this activity is for the students to use the bookmark in their next novel. Display the projects on a bulletin board in the classroom as examples so students can learn from one another.

How to Use the Activity

This activity can be used as a post-reading project on a class novel or individual novels. The size of the bookmark is determined by you. The bookmark activity sheet or construction paper works well. Students can either print, type, or use the computer to format the requested information. For a greater learning experience, the students should share the information on their bookmarks with their peers either in groups or as a class presentation (in which case the presentation can be counted as a separate grade). Upon completion of the project, students often like the idea of having the bookmarks laminated for protection.

Evaluation

The project can be evaluated by the specific criteria that you set up. A rubric can be set up so that all the bookmarks are evaluated in the same fashion. Some factors to consider are content, cleverness and originality, and completion of the assignment on time.

Variations

All information for the bookmark can be altered to emphasize whatever points need to be stressed in teaching a particular novel. One variation that requires some research is to have students look up a review or critique of the book to include, or a quote from a peer who has read the book. Bring in sample bookmarks for students to look at to get ideas for color, placement of graphics and text, and book promotion. Publishers often use bookmarks of new novels for marketing purposes, and these can be obtained by contacting the publishers.

ACTIVITY 23

BOOKMARK

Name: _____ Date: _____

Title: _____

Author: _____

Publisher and year: _____

Directions: Your project is to design a bookmark for your novel. You need to include as much of the information listed below as possible in an original, clever, colorful, and creative way. The size can be larger than the usual bookmark to make it easier to read and see.

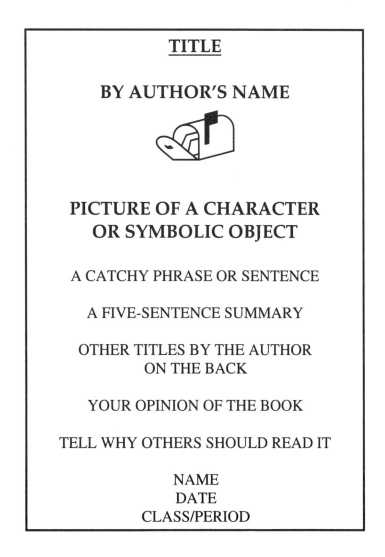

ACTIVITY 24

SCRAPBOOK FOR A CHARACTER

Purpose of the Activity

There are several purposes for this project. The first is for students to identify with a character from a novel to view well-rounded characters as real people. Students must display their understanding of a character by making a scrapbook that the character would make based on the relationships of people in the novel, decisions made in dealing with problems, and significant events that affected that character's life. The scrapbook can represent the students' insights and knowledge of a work through the eyes of a character and their interpretations of that character. The students can display their artistic and creative talents through their choices, design, and final product. Another goal is to have students share their projects with class members so they can learn from each other.

How to Use the Activity

The project can be worked on individually, in pairs, or as a group. This project can also be assigned for a class reading the same novel, with students signing up for minor characters as well as protagonists. Using several novels allows for even more variety in a discussion of books and characters. Students need to do some prewriting before beginning the project. They can make a log as they read to look for specific decisions, events, people, feelings, and objects that they might want to refer to in the scrapbook. If possible, sample photographs or scrapbooks can be used as models in the classroom. After students organize a plan or pattern for the project, they should draw, cut out, or find what they need for their scrapbooks. Having old magazines, newspapers, catalogs, and colored paper available in a supply box will help students get started and be successful. Students should label the selections within the scrapbook along with the significance of each entry. In this way, the viewer understands the significance of each item in the scrapbook.

Evaluation

The scrapbook can be evaluated as a writing project, an artistic endeavor, and a sharing experience. The standards for the evaluation should be made clear to the students at the onset of the assignment. The oral sharing and viewing of the project can be done in front of the class with a set limit of entries presented. Another possibility is to share the projects in groups where the scrapbooks are passed around and talked about. The display of the projects in the room is often a celebration of a completed event.

Variations

This activity can be used as one of several projects for students to choose from when they are asked to choose a book report or project when they finish reading a book. The power of choice gives those students who want to imagine themselves to be a character a chance to do so, while less creative students can choose something that matches their learning style.

ACTIVITY 24

SCRAPBOOK FOR A CHARACTER

Name: _____ Date: _____

Title: _____

Author: _____

Publisher and year: _____

Directions: You are to imagine that you are a character from the novel and keep a scrapbook of pictures, objects, letters, symbols, and other items that you think the character would find important enough to save in a scrapbook. The items can include pictures of other characters, important events from the plot, prize possessions, or clues to help solve a problem or mystery. The scrapbook must be bound in some fashion, and everything must be labeled with its significance.

Item	Significance
1.	
2.	
3.	
4.	
5.	
6.	
7.	
8.	
9.	
10.	

ACTIVITY 25

POSTER MAP OF THE ELEMENTS OF FICTION

Purpose of the Activity

This post-reading activity is a project that can involve all the standards of English and display students' understanding of a novel and the story elements necessary for all fiction. Six of the seven parts allow the students to write about specific elements from the story. Because the students must also use pictures and drawings, they must be analytical and choose creative, colorful graphics that also have relationships to elements in the story. Another purpose for this activity is for the students to learn from one another as they share their analyses of the novel with the class. As there are many interpretations to a novel, more than one student can read the same book and do a story map of the novel. This project allows you and class members to appreciate students' understanding of the novels they have read.

How to Use the Activity

This activity can be used with individuals, pairs, or groups. Because this project is a variation on the mapping form, the format can be changed and modified (it should be modeled before the assignment is given). Usually it is best if you first model the elements of fiction in a simpler form of literature, such as a children's book. The class can work in pairs or groups and map the elements of this story to become familiar with the terms and format before undertaking the task of mapping a novel. Decide on the size of the project; it should be put on a poster sheet that is large enough for a class presentation. The most beneficial part of representing the students' knowledge on a poster is that it will be shared with others and displayed in the classroom as an example of successful achievement.

Evaluation

This project can consist of several assessments. First, the accuracy and quality of the content can be evaluated as well as the creativity, originality, and overall appearance of the poster itself. Second, the presentation can be graded in terms of speaking and sharing the visual with others. The audience can be required to take notes or write an interesting question or insight after viewing the project.

Variations

If computers are available, students can learn how to use them to enhance the appearance of the poster. Experiment with various font styles and sizes. Graphics can be newly drawn or taken from clip art for symbols, settings, and characters if available. Placement, cutting and pasting, and layout are all important skills with this kind of format.

ACTIVITY 25

POSTER MAP OF THE ELEMENTS OF FICTION

Name: _____ Date: _____

Title: _____

Author: _____

Publisher and year: _____

Directions: Create a poster displaying the important elements of the novel. The poster should be large enough for all class members to view. The information should be represented in a concise, accurate manner. Feel free to be creative, original, and colorful.

Character (Protagonist)

In a paragraph or character map include the following:
• physical and personality description
• background information
• problems and decision-making
Try to draw or cut out a picture.

Plot

In a paragraph or sequence chart include the following:
• a short summary
• the conflict/problem
• the resolution to the problem
Draw plot diagram.

Print and Underline the Title, Author, and Publisher

New Vocabulary (1-3)
Do the following:
• print the word in large letters
• copy the sentence from the book and page #
• guess at the contextual meaning
• include the dictionary meaning and source
• write an original sentence

Symbol
Draw or cut out a picture of an object that has a special meaning in the book or that can represent the book in a symbol.

Setting
Tell where and when the story takes place
• include pictures of the most important or interesting places.

Mood
Complete three sentence that show when your feelings were strongly felt.

I felt_____ during the

part in the story when

_____.

Theme
State the message of the book in one sentence and explain it.

From *What a Novel Idea!* © 1997 Katherine Wiesolek Kuta. Teacher Ideas Press. 1-800-237-6124.

ACTIVITY 26

BOOK JACKET/BOOK COVER

Purpose of the Activity

This multipurpose activity involves students in reading, writing, and representing a work in another medium, and class members viewing the finished products in a sharing session. Students must first read a novel and then create a book cover or book jacket that would advertise the book and get others to read it. Students must use higher-level thinking, analyzing, and creative skills in order to complete this assignment. Afterward, the students will present their projects and share the information with the class. Also, they can talk about what is necessary to create a book cover or book jacket that markets the book to readers.

How to Use the Activity

The activity, which should be assigned after the book is read, offers students a chance to express themselves in a format that they may not have explored in the past. Some class discussion about layout, attractiveness, and marketing may be necessary at the onset of the project. Having sample models of novel covers and book jackets would be helpful for the students to preview. Students can then begin the project in class, or it can be assigned for homework. The cover or jacket can be cut to fit the actual book, or it can be made larger than the book for presentation purposes. You can assign a book cover alone or ask for an entire book jacket depending on how much information you want about the novel.

Evaluation

Because this activity covers so many skills, it can be graded in a variety of ways. The students should be told exactly how they will be assessed on the activity. Certainly the writing and the literal and inferential information should be accurate. The design and attractiveness of the cover/jacket can also be assessed. Meeting a deadline is an important factor as well. If the project was done cooperatively, the cooperative group work can be considered. Finally, sharing can be a separate grade.

Variations

Computer graphics and text can be incorporated into the cover/jacket. Also, students can draw the cover themselves. Others can cut out pictures to represent ideas. You can use the idea of creating book covers as a springboard for students' written work at any time.

ACTIVITY 26

BOOK JACKET/BOOK COVER

Name: _____ Date: _____

Title: _____

Author: _____

Publisher and year: _____

Directions: Create a book jacket/book cover as assigned following the format below.
Look at sample book covers and sample book jackets in the library. Your project must be informative as well as attractive.

(cover)

ONE-SENTENCE PLOT OR CATCHY PHRASE   ARTISTIC DRAWING OF CHARACTERS AND/OR SYMBOLIC OBJECTS AUTHOR, PUBLISHER, AND YEAR

(jacket back cover)

SHORT PLOT SUMMARY TELL APPEAL OF BOOK TO READERS

(inside flaps of jacket)

POSSIBLE CHOICES: BOOK REVIEW AUTHOR'S BACKGROUND CHARACTER DESCRIPTION OTHER STUDENT OPINIONS IMPORTANT QUOTATIONS POSSIBLE THEMES

ACTIVITY 27

COMIC STRIP BASED ON PLOT AND THEME

Purpose of the Activity

This representing/viewing activity offers the opportunity for students to be creative and artistic as they display their understanding of an important event in the novel. They will not only condense the events into a comic strip format but also will explain, in writing, the message in the drawings. Additionally, the students will represent the literary form of the novel in a different medium. If you have them share their work with others, their classmates will gain a deeper understanding of the novel.

How to Use the Activity

This activity would probably be most appropriate after the novel is finished, but the students can record significant events or situations in a journal as they read to refer to when they are done. They must then choose an event or situation to portray in the comic strip that they feel holds the most meaning for the novel: a turning point, a character's decision, or an exciting plot event. You can set the parameters of the assignment and the number of comic strip frames as desired.

Evaluation

Because many students are not artistically inclined, stick figures should be acceptable as people, and details may be sparse. Your assessment should be in the accuracy of the events portrayed and the reasoning for the choice of events. The interpretation is also a key element to consider in grading. The sharing in pairs, groups, or the entire class can also be graded and can provoke class discussion and questions.

Variations

Ask the students to draw a comic strip that portrays the future of a character, or to make predictions about the plotline at the conclusion of the novel. This activity can also be given as one of several for students to choose from as an alternative book project. Students who are artistically talented will have the opportunity to display their skills and succeed with the book project.

ACTIVITY 27

COMIC STRIP BASED ON PLOT AND THEME

Name: _____ Date: _____

Title: _____

Author: _____

Publisher and year: _____

Directions: Choose an event that holds the most meaning for the novel, such as a turning point, a character's decision, or a prediction in the plotline. Create a comic strip based on this event.

EVENT	**EVENT**

EVENT	**EVENT**

LESSON/MORAL/THEME/INFERENCE OF THIS STRIP

ACTIVITY 28

MURAL OF SYMBOLIC PLOT SEQUENCES

Purpose of the Activity

There are several purposes for this representing/viewing activity. The first is for students to think at an interpretative level and show their understanding of the novel with pictorial representations of characters and events. Second, the students must work cooperatively in order to successfully discuss the main events of the book, decide how to artistically create events in symbols, and complete the project on time to present it to the class as a visual. Third, students will present their mural to the class and explain the drawings, apply the symbols to life, and relate the significance of the events they portray to the novel and its themes. The class will view the mural and listen to the share sessions to learn about the book and their peers' interpretations.

How to Use the Activity

This activity can be assigned to a class reading the same novel or to a class reading individual novels. This activity can also be offered as one of several choices of projects from this book for students who like expressing themselves through art. Butcher block paper can be used for a larger version of a mural, or standard-size paper can be taped together to create a miniature wall hanging. The students must have an understanding of symbols, plot sequence, themes, and murals to undertake this activity. Possibly a class discussion or research can be conducted to increase students' knowledge in these areas. An art teacher can be a resource for ideas on artwork, the elements of a mural, and models. You need to decide the parameters of the assignment. Students can work in pairs, groups, or an entire class if the class is small. The number of significant sections of the novel must be discussed and outlined before the project begins. It is advisable to do sketches separately before doing a final copy. One possibility is to make sections on the mural by chapters, major episodes, or the events of the plot triangle (exposition, rising action, climax, falling action, and resolution). The ability of the students as well as their number determines the restrictions of the project.

Evaluation

The evaluation can include the preparation, working process, cooperative attitude, final product, and presentation. This project can be considered a formal activity, and each individual/pair/group can be held responsible for a particular part of the mural.

Variations

Once a class has completed a mural, keep it as a model if the project is repeated in the future. The mural's format can be thematic, sequential, chronological, character growth, or a combination of the novel's events paralleled with the historical events. The format for the mural depends on the structure of the novel.

ACTIVITY 28

MURAL OF SYMBOLIC PLOT SEQUENCES

Name: _____ Date: _____

Title: _____

Author: _____

Publisher and year: _____

Directions: Create a wall mural displaying the plot by chapters or episodes. Use this form to plan the mural.

ACTIVITY 29

AUTHOR PROMOTION POSTER

Purpose of the Activity

This activity involves students in reading, writing, researching, representing, and sharing, and an audience in viewing. Students can read one or more of an author's books. Then they research information about the author and her or his works. The students then will represent important information about the author in the form of an attractive visual poster for class members to view so that they too can learn about the author. This activity reminds students that writers are real people with real lives and real problems.

How to Use the Activity

This activity would be most successful if all class members or groups were assigned individual writers to research and produced a poster to share. If class members are reading books of their choice, this project would be ideal for students to become familiar with many writers and types of literature. This project can also be used as a means for teaching the research and inquiry process, where the students write questions for which they would like answers. Students should look in a variety of sources in the library and, if available, can also use technology for searches. They must gather and sort through materials to choose information about an author that answers their initial questions, and they must be able to synthesize, condense, and write main ideas that are interesting and informative for a specific audience. The class members can log main ideas in a notebook for future reference, which is also a form of note-taking practice.

Evaluation

The entire process can have several points for assessment as students participate in and complete the various steps of the research. If the students work independently, the final product and formal presentation can be graded. The class members' notes can be assessed, and the importance of meeting a deadline should be stressed.

Variations

This activity can be offered as one of several projects for students to choose from as a book or author report. The format and information requested on the sample are only a model to get students started. When the project begins, the students can write their initial questions on the poster, and later they can explain how they arrived at their conclusions.

ACTIVITY 29

AUTHOR PROMOTION POSTER

Name: _____ Date: _____

Title: _____

Author: _____

Publisher and year: _____

Directions: Create a poster about your novel's author that includes the information below.

Background Information:
- Who is the person?
- What is important to know about this person?
- Where does or did this person live?
- When did this person write?
- Why is this person successful as a writer?

Picture of Author

Author's Name

Symbol for Author

List Other Writings

Explain why you admire this author.

ACTIVITY 30

MOBILE OF CHARACTERS

Purpose of the Activity

The main purpose of this representing/viewing project is for students to display information about their novel in a creative mobile that can be hung in the classroom for all students to view. Students will learn about the characters in the novel through the use of symbol shapes and concise wording on each shape. Students must plan and prepare a project that is visually appealing as well as informative.

How to Use the Activity

This activity can be offered as one of several projects for students to choose from in this book. Students who are creative, draw, and like a hands-on activity can choose to complete this assignment. The activity can also be used on a class novel or several different books for variety. Students will need to take notes on several characters as they read to gather information for this project. Because not all the information can be used in the predetermined amount of space, the students must be selective and choose the most important facts that make a character different from others. You can direct the students to the kinds of information needed for character understanding. Using different shapes will help students realize that each character is unique in his/her own way. There should be a reason why a particular shape is chosen for a character. One side of the shape should house a picture, and the other side of the shape should contain information about the character. The shapes can be enlarged or altered if necessary. Students will punch holes in each shape and hang them from a coat hanger, rod, or piece of wood. Display the projects in the classroom for all students. Part of this assignment is to have the students share their projects with other class members.

Evaluation

The project assessment can include the degree of creativity, the ability to meet a deadline, content, and a presentation.

Variations

These same shapes can be used to display the elements of plot, characters, setting, mood, and theme for a novel. Through using different shapes, the students realize that each element is unique but necessary for every story.

ACTIVITY 30

MOBILE OF CHARACTERS

Name: _____ Date: _____

Title: _____

Author: _____

Publisher and year: _____

Directions: Create a mobile based on the characters in the novel. Each character must have a picture or drawing to show your interpretation of the character's appearance. On the other side of the symbolic shape there should be pertinent information about the character's life, background, family, values, behavior, problems, friends, growth or learning in the novel, and other items of interest. These symbolic shapes can be cut and attached to a coat hanger or other stable item. The pieces can hang from string, ribbon, or strips of material.

Be prepared to share your project with the class in a formal presentation.

Names of Characters:

1.

2.

3.

4.

5.

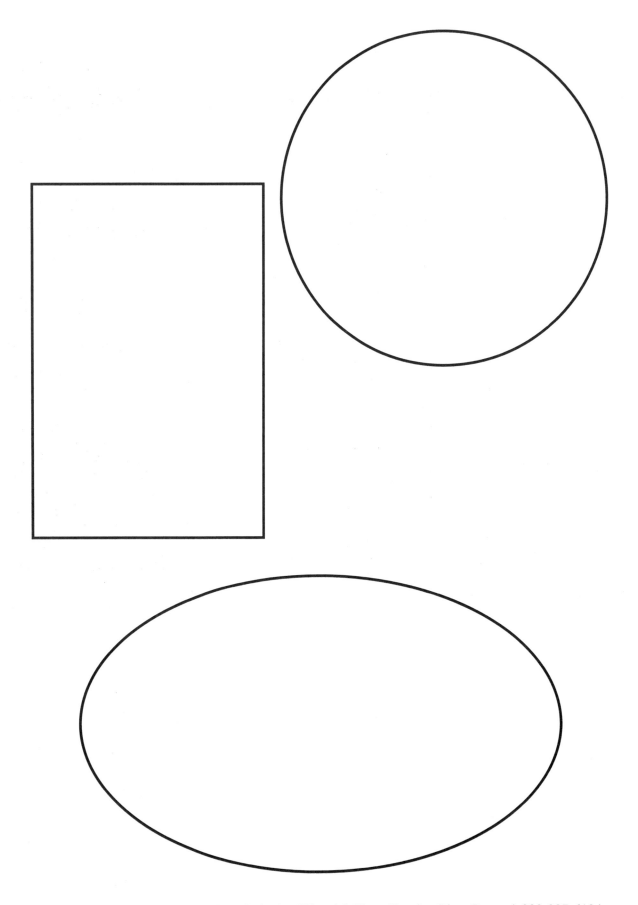

ACTIVITY 31

AWARD CERTIFICATE FOR A CHARACTER

Purpose of the Activity

The purpose of this representing/viewing activity is for students to analytically decide which character from a novel deserves a certificate award for heroic traits. Students must create an award stating both literal and inferential information. Another purpose of this activity is for students to express themselves in writing by giving reasons to justify their choice of candidate. Upon presenting the award for class members to view, students will discuss the idea of a hero and heroic traits.

How to Use the Activity

The award activity can be used as a model for students so that they can create their own award with whatever design they feel is appropriate. Students can practice prewriting, writing a rough draft, and editing before making a final product. Students should also supply a persuasive theme convincing the audience that the character deserves such an award.

Evaluation

Students can be assessed while working on the writing process and on the final award. A formal persuasive speech can also be set up for evaluation, or informal sharing can be done in groups or pairs.

Variations

Students can brainstorm the kinds of awards that people receive and the standards necessary to be an award recipient. They can create awards for other characters for different reasons. This project can be suggested as one of several projects for students to choose from to report on their novel. Students can create other kinds of awards for characters in the novels, such as "Best Friend Award," "Best Parent Award," or "Best Problem Solver." This activity can spark all kinds of discussion on awards and the qualities needed for public recognition.

ACTIVITY 31

AWARD CERTIFICATE FOR A CHARACTER

Name: _____ Date: _____

Title: _____

Author: _____

Publisher and year: _____

Directions: Create an award for a character in your novel if you feel that he or she deserves an award for his or her heroic deeds. If a character deserves an award for some other special quality or deed, you can change the title to one more appropriate than the model given. Use the space below to justify the reasons this person should receive an award, giving specific examples from the book (in the form of a well-written paragraph) to support your decision.

Name of Award Recipient: _____

Title of Award: _____

_____

Reason for Award: _____

_____

_____

_____

_____

_____

_____

_____

_____

_____

CERTIFICATE OF ACHIEVEMENT

Awarded to

_____

In Recognition of These Accomplishments:

_____
_____
_____
_____
_____

Given the ____ day of _____ , in the year ____

by

_____

From *What a Novel Idea!* © 1997 Katherine Wiesolek Kuta. Teacher Ideas Press. 1-800-237-6124.

ACTIVITY 32

COMPARISON/CONTRAST CHART OF CHARACTERS

Purpose of the Activity

There are several purposes for this representing/viewing activity. It gives students the opportunity to write, to represent their knowledge in a chart, and to have their classmates view their projects. Students will use higher thinking skills to compare and contrast one character to another and/or to themselves. By studying similarities and differences between characters, students will understand the many differences but also similarities among people. This can open a discussion about empathy for people and their problems. Students will present and share their information either formally or informally with class members. Finally, the class will view a visual chart and listen to their peers' ideas.

How to Use the Activity

This activity can be used for the entire class, or it can be offered as one of several activities from this book to students. Students can complete this activity during reading or afterward. The activity requires the students to look beyond the text for similarities and differences. Students need to find specific examples to support their generalizations and observations. The graphic organizer can be used as a rough draft. A final draft can become a larger visual for the presentation if students are to practice presentation skills. Some elements for comparison include personality, parents, hobbies, interests, schooling, problems, appearance, background, friends, relationships, and likes and dislikes.

Evaluation

This activity can be evaluated in a number of ways. It can be assessed as a class or homework activity, a written assignment, or a presentation. The amount or credit given for an assignment depends on the time and purpose of the project.

Variations

Students can create their own charts for comparisons and contrasts between two minor characters, two novels, or two elements within a novel. These charts can also be used as graphic organizers to help students marshal their ideas and information before a more complex written assignment is given. A column could be changed on the chart and the student's name added so that a character's trait can be compared and contrasted to a real person.

ACTIVITY 32

COMPARISON/CONTRAST CHART OF CHARACTERS

Name: _____ Date: _____

Title: _____

Author: _____

Publisher and year: _____

Directions: Create a chart to share with the class that compares similarities and contrasts differences for two characters in the novel. Support your choices with examples from the text.

Same or Different?   How?

Item Discussed	First Character's Name	Second Character's Name	How? Examples
1.			
2.			
3.			
4.			
5.			

ACTIVITY 33

VOCABULARY MAPPING

Purpose of the Activity

The first purpose for this activity is to have students increase their vocabulary by interacting with new words in context. The second purpose is for the students to assume responsibility for their learning by choosing words that they are unfamiliar with as they read. The third is that the students will learn from each other by presentations of words in class. Fourth, students will practice thinking symbolically to help increase memory and to help make connections to their lives.

How to Use the Activity

There are several ways to use this graphic organizer. One is for students to find a certain number of words to map as they read. You can pass out the required number of forms to the students for mapping. Another suggestion is for each student to find and share one word for class members to take notes on, thus creating a class list of vocabulary enhancement. This form can also be used as a model for students to use for a poster presentation on their vocabulary word.

Evaluation

Students can be assessed on their ability to meet a deadline, to create a map with accurate information on a word, and to share information by practicing their presentation skills. One method of testing a group of class vocabulary words is for you to use the students' sentences for a quiz and ask students to match a list of words with the correct blanks in the sentences. Students will need to use contextual skills to choose which vocabulary word makes sense in each sentence. Another form of testing includes using just the student-drawn pictures for matching with the class vocabulary words.

Variations

You can vary the requested information on a word if you are stressing antonyms, homonyms, etymology, or dictionary skills. You can also request that the students use a number of vocabulary words in a specific writing assignment or one of the suggested activity book projects. The more exposure students have to the vocabulary, the more likely the words will become part of their everyday language.

ACTIVITY 33

VOCABULARY MAPPING

Name: _____ Date: _____

Title: _____

Author: _____

Publisher and year: _____

Write the contextual definition,
then check for the dictionary definition   Write your own sentence

_____   _____

_____   _____

_____   _____

Write the word, page number, and part of speech

_____

_____

_____

Write one or two synonyms   Draw or find a picture to represent the word

_____

_____

ACTIVITY 34

COMPARISON/CONTRAST CHART FOR A NOVEL AND MOVIE

Purpose of the Activity

First, the students must read the novel and view the movie. Then the students must record information in a chart that requires familiarity with literary terms. This activity has students using higher-level thinking skills to compare and contrast specific points and deciding whether the two media are similar to or different from each other and how. The students will make judgments and support their answers and choices. They will discuss their choices after reading and viewing the two media.

How to Use the Activity

The students can complete the chart while they read, or all three columns can be completed after reading and viewing the movie. This activity would work successfully with groups, pairs, or individuals depending on the ability of the group and your purpose. One advantage of having students work cooperatively is that they can be given roles for which they are responsible and a specific task to complete. Members should share openly but be dependent on each other for the success of the task. Some possible roles are organizer, recorder, reporter, and timekeeper.

Evaluation

Students can be assessed for their observations and analyses of the two art forms. You can allow students to work in pairs to assist each other. This activity can be graded as a class assignment, formal written report, or graphic organizer presentation. The main focus should be that students explain, with details, the reasons for their answers.

Variations

Alter the form to emphasize other points. A comparison/contrast chart can also be used between two novels of a genre or author.

ACTIVITY 34

COMPARISON/CONTRAST CHART FOR A NOVEL AND MOVIE

Name: _____ Date: _____

Title of novel: _____

Author: _____

Publisher and year: _____

Title of movie: _____

Directions: Find a movie that has been made from your novel, or find a movie that is very similar to your book, and record the similarities and differences.

CHARACTERISTIC	NOVEL	MOVIE	SIMILAR OR DIFFERENT AND HOW
PLOT LINE (ONE SENTENCE)			
PROTAGONIST			
SETTING			
CONFLICTS/ PROBLEMS			
THEME			
MOOD			
POINT OF VIEW			
READER'S OR VIEWER'S OPINION			
RATING IN STARS (1-5) AND WHY			

ACTIVITY 35

TIMELINE OF THE EVENTS OF THE PLOT

Purpose of the Activity

The purpose of this activity is for students to choose important events from the novel and arrange them in sequential order using words and symbolic pictures. The students must also explain the significance of the events and reasons why they were chosen for the timeline. The students will represent the novel in a format that requires them to use higher thinking skills in order to analyze, find, and sequentially arrange objects to represent actions in the book. The students will share their timelines with the class for discussion.

How to Use the Activity

Students can keep a journal as they read so that they can record important events and significant symbolism. Then they can use their notes to choose the most important events that cover the plot from exposition through resolution. The events should be labeled below the horizontal timeline in concise words. Above the timeline, the students should draw or place pictorial symbols that represent each event in the sequence of the plot. Students can write, orally present, or do both and share with the class their choices and the significance of the events in the book.

Evaluation

Students' projects can be assessed in several ways or in just one manner. Depending on what you choose to focus on with this activity, the students can be evaluated for their sequencing skills, writing skills, content information, speaking skills, or all four. The students must be aware of the emphasis at the beginning of the project.

Variations

Enlarge the timeline so the students can create a visual for class presentation. You can also add or subtract the number of events requested on the timeline. A possible prewriting activity is for students to practice working with a timeline by placing important events in their lives in sequence and bringing symbolic objects that represent those moments in their lives.

ACTIVITY 35

TIMELINE OF THE EVENTS OF THE PLOT

Name: _____ Date: _____

Title: _____

Author: _____

Publisher and year: _____

Directions: Display the important events from the novel in sequential order. Use words below the line and pictures above the line. On a separate piece of paper, explain the significance of the events and the reasons why you chose these particular events.

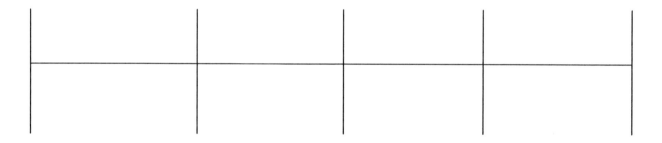

ACTIVITY 36

TRAVEL BROCHURE FOR A SETTING

Purpose of the Activity

This activity emphasizes representing/viewing standards. Students should be original and imaginative in creating a brochure about a setting (fictional or real) used in a novel. They will need to view professional travel books and brochures to get ideas for their own projects, and they will need to research the settings to find accurate information to include in their brochures. Students will share their projects with their classmates and increase their knowledge of the novel.

How to Use the Activity

This activity can be assigned to an entire class or offered as one of several choices from this book. Artistic students often find this a golden opportunity for them to display their learning style. Because some prior knowledge about travel brochure formats, places in the world, and art layout is necessary, students should do some research into the settings used in their novel, visit a travel agency, or talk with an art teacher. Students can brainstorm the kind of information needed to make a travel brochure attractive to customers. They should plan their designs before drawing and writing. Using a computer with different fonts and graphics would make the brochures very attractive, and students would become acquainted with desktop publishing. Drawn or cut-out pictures are equally acceptable. When the project is done, the students can share their work formally in a presentation or informally in round-table groups. They can relate what they learned from this creative experience and some interesting details about the setting. They can also explain the reasons the author chose that particular setting for the novel and its relationship to the entire novel.

Evaluation

This project can be assessed in stages. The research and preliminary planning process can be evaluated as well as the final product. Students can assess each other's brochures by deciding which places they would like to visit and their reasons for choosing those places.

Variations

Students can be given a specific format to follow or a certain setting to promote if they need more structure. Students can also practice writing business letters to travel bureaus requesting information on a particular place in the book. They can use the information for the brochure and expand their background knowledge of the book as well.

ACTIVITY 36

TRAVEL BROCHURE FOR A SETTING

Name: _____ Date: _____

Title: _____

Author: _____

Publisher and year: _____

Directions: Create a travel brochure advertising the setting, the where and the when, used in the novel. The brochure should be attractive and informative so someone would consider visiting the setting (even though it may be totally fictional).

Setting Where: _____ When: _____

ACTIVITY 37

POSTCARD FROM ONE CHARACTER TO ANOTHER

Purpose of the Activity

There are several purposes for this activity, which involves reading, writing, representing, and viewing. First, the students must read a novel and understand a character well enough to assume the identity of that character and write a postcard to another character in the story. Second, the students will use their writing skills to concisely communicate some ideas about significant actions, decisions, and observations in the book. Third, the students will represent the novel in another form that displays their interpretations of character and plot. Fourth, the class members will view each other's work to gain more insight into the characters and the thought processes of other students.

How to Use the Activity

You can assign this project to a class or offer it as one of several to choose from. Show the class sample postcards for models and discuss reasons why people communicate in this manner. Large index cards would allow students to draw a picture of a setting in the book and use the other side for the message and address. The form of the postcard in this book can be enlarged if the emphasis is only on writing. After students produce postcards, they can share them with classmates and explain the significance of the communication in relation to the book.

Evaluation

Students can be evaluated for the written portion of the project (the message), for following the directions and format properly, for maintaining accuracy of detail, for meeting a deadline, for being creative, and for sharing the project with others.

Variations

To help direct students, you can suggest the topic of the message or offer several choices for students. You can also dictate which character is writing to which other character.

ACTIVITY 37

POSTCARD FROM ONE CHARACTER TO ANOTHER

Name: _____ Date: _____

Title: _____

Author: _____

Publisher and year: _____

Directions: Imagine that you are one of the characters in the book. You plan to write a postcard to another character in the book. Remember to stay in character and discuss events, problems, and insights.

Date	Stamp
Message	Fictional Address of Character
Signed by character	

ACTIVITY 38

BUMPER STICKER

Purpose of the Activity

There are several purposes for this activity. The most important one is that the students will pass along positive themes, inspiring motifs, or words of wisdom from a book in the form of a bumper sticker. The students must brainstorm before actually writing their message in a concise, clear manner. Then the students must defend their choices with examples from the text and apply their messages to the real world. Finally, students will present their bumper sticker to the class for critique and questions.

How to Use the Activity

In this activity students are asked to brainstorm universal themes, motifs, or words of wisdom from their novel. The purpose of a bumper sticker can be discussed, and sample bumper stickers can be used as models so the students can get a better idea why people put stickers on cars. The students must select the best saying, theme, etc. that is appropriate for placement on a bumper sticker and that will affect viewers positively. They will then place this saying on an attractive bumper sticker for display in the classroom. Additionally, they must explain in writing the significance of the insight in their novel and its universality. The students can share in groups or with the entire class.

Evaluation

This project can be evaluated in terms of students' abilities to meet a deadline, to complete an assignment, to follow directions, to be creative, to explain the message as it relates to the novel and life, and to present the project in a clear manner.

Variations

Students can discuss other forms of communication that people use to get ideas across in public places. They can also choose a bumper sticker from the class's presentations and write about how it applies to their life.

ACTIVITY 38

BUMPER STICKER

Name: _____ Date: _____

Title: _____

Author: _____

Publisher and year: _____

Directions: Think of a clever, universal, insightful message from your novel that would be appropriate to place on a car bumper for others to read: words of wisdom for others to live by. Explain how the message is universal and how it applies to your novel, with specific examples.

[blank box]

Significance: _____

_____

_____

_____

_____

ACTIVITY 39

GREETING CARD

Purpose of the Activity

This activity has students assuming the identity of a character in order to write a greeting card to another character. Students must first understand the variety of reasons why people write and send cards to others. Then the students must choose a specific purpose, decide on characters, and find a situation in the novel where one character might have sent a card to the other. The students will make assumptions, based on facts and events in the book, about how sending the card would have changed the plot, and they will write their explanation with supporting details from the text. Finally, the class members will view all the cards and listen to the explanations by the students to share their interpretations.

How to Use the Activity

This post-reading project would be most successfully completed by individuals. Allow students to preview a variety of greeting cards and discuss the kinds of cards that they might have received. A discussion of the types of cards and their purposes would also connect prior knowledge to the project. The teachers can ask students to prewrite about several situations, character relationships, and critical decision points in the novel that may lend themselves to this form of communication. Students can also discuss letters, cards, or other communications that have affected their lives. The form can be enlarged for students to write on directly, or pieces of paper can be folded in half to create any number of cards. Students always enjoy and learn by sharing each other's projects in class, either formally or informally.

Evaluation

This project can be graded in terms of the greeting card, fulfilling requirements, and the written explanation of the card's relationship to the characters and events in the novel.

Variations

Ask students to respond to the greeting card in some way. They can also make judgments as to whether the various cards would actually have affected a character's decisions or plot events. They can rank cards according to their appropriateness and effectiveness.

ACTIVITY 39

GREETING CARD

Name: _____ Date: _____

Title: _____

Author: _____

Publisher and year: _____

Directions: Choose a greeting card format and imagine that one character is sending a card to another character in the novel. Then explain the importance of this choice and how it could have affected action in the novel if the card had actually been sent.

Choices of Cards: Birthday, Sympathy, Thank You, Get Well, Friendship, Anniversary, Retirement, New Baby, Valentine's Day, Christmas, Miss You.

Choice of Card: _____

From: _____ **To:** _____

(Front)	(Inside)

ACTIVITY 40

FORTUNE COOKIE SAYINGS FOR THE CHARACTERS

Purpose of the Activity

In this representing and viewing activity, students must write a brief and concise message for each important character that would be appropriate according to their past, present, or future lives. Thus, the purposes of the activity are for students to display understanding of character, to make inferences based on details and facts from the novel, to write briefly and concisely, to be creative, and to have fun. This activity also gives students the opportunity to share or present their work so classmates can learn from it.

How to Use the Activity

This activity can be used as a post-reading project for a class novel or individually chosen books. If the term "fortune cookie" is not generally known to the students, you can explain it. Actual fortune cookies can be brought into the classroom as examples. Students can use the real fortunes as models or even match them with characters from the novel.

Evaluation

The assessment depends on the emphasis that you want to place on the activity. This activity can be used as a class activity or as an actual book project. Students can make a presentation on one or more of the fortunes and offer an extensive explanation for the match of a fortune and a character.

Variations

Have the students randomly choose a fortune from a hat, match it to a character in the book if possible, and explain why the fortune matches that character or why it doesn't match any character. The fortunes can also be used for more extensive essay writing for a theme or test.

ACTIVITY 40

FORTUNE COOKIE SAYINGS FOR THE CHARACTERS

Name: _____ Date: _____

Title: _____

Author: _____

Publisher and year: _____

Directions: Write a prediction or saying for each main character that is appropriate for that person based on your reading of the novel. Make sure you explain the relationship of the sayings to the characters.

FORTUNE 1

Character's Name and Explanation

_____

FORTUNE 2

Character's Name and Explanation

_____

FORTUNE 3

Character's Name and Explanation

_____

FORTUNE 4

Character's Name and Explanation

_____

FORTUNE 5

Character's Name and Explanation

_____

Speaking and Listening
Standards Activities

ACTIVITY 41

ONE-MINUTE BOOKTALK

Purpose of the Activity

This activity emphasizes speaking and listening skills that will give students the opportunity to share their knowledge of the novel with class members. Other students will learn about new titles and authors that they might want to sample. Because all the students are members of the audience, they can practice appropriate listening skills by being courteous, attentive, and supportive during the booktalks. Finally, students will sharpen their speaking skills in front of an audience.

How to Use the Activity

This activity can be used when a class reads a variety of novels or individuals have presentations to share with the class. Usually all class members can share their novels within one or two class periods. Students can refer to note cards but should not be allowed to simply read the information on the cards to the class. Generally, students find this booktalk format less threatening than longer speeches, and they are often eager to present their projects in this manner if a written project is also due.

Evaluation

Because this activity is an informal sharing of information or a project, you may want to grade the speech informally by giving credit for sharing and following the directions or no credit for being unprepared or unwilling to share. Students worry less if the emphasis is not on the speech but on the willingness to share a book with others.

Variations

Students can sit in a circle to share if the class is small, or several circles to share in groups. You can vary the information that is asked for in the booktalk. If booktalks are used often, students become familiar with speaking to the class, which prepares them for more formal presentations later.

ACTIVITY 41

ONE-MINUTE BOOKTALK

Name: _____ Date: _____

Title: _____

Author: _____

Publisher and year: _____

Suggested Outline of Topics for Presentation Sharing or Novel Sharing

1. Hold up the book for the class members to view and name the title, author, publisher, and year of publication of the novel.

2. Tell a short summary of the plot in about five sentences to give an overview of the basic type of book and the events within.

3. Describe the main character (protagonist), using three to five relevant adjectives, and explain whether that person is someone you would like as a friend, or why you would not like that person as a friend.

4. State the theme of the story in one sentence. Explain how you learned this overall message.

5. Critique the book by saying who should read the book in the future and giving reasons why you liked or disliked the novel.

6. If there is a project involved, explain the significance of the project and its relationship to the novel.

Optional:

Share a new, interesting, or unusual vocabulary word with the class. Write the word on the chalkboard, say it, give the definition, and use it in a sentence.

ACTIVITY 42

A BOOK IN A WEEK

Purpose of the Activity

This activity involves listening and speaking standards. Its purpose is for students to work cooperatively as a class to read a portion of a novel and share information to create a basic familiarity with the characters and plot among all class members. Hopefully students will become interested enough to read the book in its entirety, or even another title by the same author. This activity is also a motivational one for students who think they cannot read an entire book; here, they cover an entire book in a school week.

How to Use the Activity

The directions are stated on the activity sheet. This activity can also be used as a motivational activity to begin a novel unit, to introduce a genre type, to add variety when teaching about an author, or to teach plot structure. The students are always surprised that a teacher would tear up a book to pass out chapters; this action certainly gets their attention! The chapters can be stapled and saved for reuse after the activity is over. You must be prepared to speak about chapters when students are absent or unprepared so that the plot flows in sequence. There can be no makeup for students in this type of activity.

Steps to Follow

Choose a book that has enough chapters for all students or for students to work in pairs. The book must be readable by all class members. Tear the book into chapters. For effect and to stress the need to save time and work cooperatively, you may want to tear the chapters in front of the class.

Read the first and possibly the second chapter to the class out loud. Give each student or pair a chapter and a copy of the table of contents. Have the students read their chapters and take notes as stated on the activity sheet to share with the class. If possible, the students should get in a circle and talk about their chapter.

Everyone listens without interrupting. You may request that students take notes on plot events and characters. Read the last chapter or two aloud at completion of the sharing.

Have students write a summary of the plot based on what they heard. They should discuss and evaluate the process of reading a book in this fashion.

Evaluation

The assessment can take into consideration the students' ability to follow directions, share information, and listen to or take notes on what other students share. Evaluation of the summary writing and critiquing of the activity can take place at the conclusion of the sharing. Students can also be asked to write a one-sentence theme stating the message of the novel or what they learned from the book.

Variations

The amount of information requested for each chapter can be lengthened depending on the time you want to allow for the chapter presentations. Remember, the longer the sharing goes on, the higher the risk of students being absent and being unable to follow the plot sequence. Also, ask students to pick out one or two words in context to share in their presentation, and have the class keep a list of these words for testing later.

ACTIVITY 42

A BOOK IN A WEEK

Name: _____ Date: _____

Title: _____

Author: _____

Publisher and year: _____

Directions: Once you have received your chapter, read it and take notes as stated below to share with the class. During the presentations, listen without interrupting. After the book is finished, write a summary of the plot and be prepared to discuss and evaluate the process of reading a book in this manner.

Guidelines for Note Taking on Each Chapter

1. Give a short summary of what happens in the chapter, including new characters that are introduced.

2. Try to predict what you think is going to happen in the next chapter.

3. What questions would you like answered in later chapters?

ACTIVITY 43

CREATE A POEM ON A THEME OR FEELING

Purpose of the Activity

This creative writing activity not only involves the reading of a novel and the writing of poetry, but it also has students share their ideas and feelings with other class members. This project covers the standards of reading, writing, speaking, and listening. The students also learn new forms of poetry, and they must make connections between poetry and prose by writing about universal themes and feelings.

How to Use the Activity

This post-reading activity would be most successful if students worked individually to express their feelings and relate their own experiences to the novel and their poems. This activity can also be used in conjunction with a poetry unit. Students need to see similarities between the themes of different genres. You can assign this activity to students who have all read the same book or who have read individual books. The activity can be offered as one of several projects from this book for students to choose according to their learning strengths.

Evaluation

This activity can be assessed as other writing and sharing projects are assessed. Grades can be given for the writing portion and for the speaking/sharing portion. Other factors to take into consideration are the ability to meet a deadline, to follow directions, to format the poems correctly, and to explain the theme and its relationship to the novel and poems.

Variations

The students can illustrate their poems and thus create a visual aid for their presentation. You can choose how many and what kinds of poems are required for the project. There are many more types of poems the students could try than the ones suggested, which were chosen because they are short and fun and have easy formats to follow. Other, more difficult forms include the sonnet, ballad, and narrative poem.

ACTIVITY 43

CREATE A POEM ON A THEME OR FEELING

Name: _____ Date: _____

Title: _____

Author: _____

Publisher and year: _____

Directions: Write two or three poems whose meanings contain a universal theme or truth similar to the theme of your novel. You can follow the form of one of the poetry types listed below, or you can write free verse.

Universal Message from Novel:

_____

_____.

Poem Suggestions: Haiku, Concrete Picture Poem, Limerick, Metonymy, Cinquain, or Free Verse

Haiku   Title: _____

    line 1 - 5 syllables

    line 2 - 7 syllables

    line 3 - 5 syllables

_____

_____

_____

Concrete Poem   Title: _____

A concrete poem creates an actual picture through the placement of the words.

Limerick   Title: _____

    line 1 - (a)
    line 2 - (a)
    line 3 - (b)
    line 4 - (b)
    line 5 - (a)

Lines 1, 2, and 5 rhyme, and lines 3 and 4 are usually shorter.

_____

_____

_____

_____

_____

Metonymy   Title: _____

Another name for this poem type is a definition poem. The title is an abstract word or concept that is defined with images that have no particular pattern.

_____

_____

_____

_____

_____

Cinquain   Title:_____

This poem has two patterns of five lines each; either one is correct to follow.

    line 1 - 2 syllables (the topic)
    line 2 - 4 syllables (describes the topic)
    line 3 - 6 syllables (action words—verbs)
    line 4 - 8 syllables (a feeling or emotion)
    line 5 - 2 syllables (a synonym for the title)

    line 1 - 1 word (a noun—thing)
    line 2 - 2 words (adjectives—tell what kind, how many, or which one)
    line 3 - 3 words (verbs—show action)
    line 4 - 4 words (a phrase about it)
    line 5 - 5 words (a synonym for the noun)

_____

_____

_____

_____

_____

Free Verse   Title: _____

This type of poetry does not contain rhyme or any particular pattern.

_____

_____

_____

_____

_____

_____

_____

ACTIVITY 44

CREATE A SONG ON A THEME OF A BOOK

Purpose of Activity

This activity allows students to display their creative talents by writing lyrics for a song. Students will learn the difficult process of writing words that connect with music. They must also share their ideas and feelings with others so they can practice speaking skills, and the audience members can practice their listening skills. Both speakers and listeners learn to appreciate each other.

How to Use the Activity

This post-reading activity can be worked on individually or in pairs. You can decide how many stanzas there should be and how long they are. Students can discuss creative artists and the process of writing lyrics and music. Some students may already be familiar with writing music and playing instruments and can share their insights. Because some students may feel uncomfortable about writing lyrics if they do not like music, this activity can be offered as one of several to choose from. Sample songs can be played in class so the students can discuss the messages and feelings brought out in music.

Evaluation

Although this activity involves writing, the primary emphasis is on the presentation of the lyrics to the class. The students should understand the assessment process (as defined by you) at the beginning of the assignment. A major consideration is the connection between the lyrics and the novel.

Variations

Ask students to bring songs that have a similar theme or feeling to the novel under discussion, and have the students explain the connections of the songs and novel to their own lives.

ACTIVITY 44

CREATE A SONG ON A THEME OF A BOOK

Name: _____ Date: _____

Title: _____

Author: _____

Publisher and year: _____

Directions: Write a song that has the same message or theme as the novel. You can just write the lyrics, or you can substitute your lyrics into a particular song. Be prepared to share your project with the class.

Theme: _____

Relationship to Novel: _____

_____

Name of Song: _____

Background Music: _____

Lyrics: _____

_____

_____

_____

_____

_____

_____

_____

_____

ACTIVITY 45

SHARE RESPONSES ON A NOVEL

Purpose of the Activity

The purpose of this activity is for students to read, write, speak, and listen to not only the text but also each other in class. This activity asks students to make connections during or after the reading process and write ideas down. Then they interact with their classmates and respond to one another's questions to help make the text more understandable to each other. By having the students read a question and response aloud, other students must listen and will gain further insights into the book.

How to Use the Activity

Class members will write three questions or comments on index cards (or on three slips of paper cut from the worksheet) while they are reading their novel or after they finish. (Students should be familiar with journal or response writing.) The students' cards are shuffled and distributed randomly to class members, who will write the question, the name of the person who wrote the question, and an answer or response to the question in the boxes on the worksheet. The students then choose the most valuable question or response to read aloud. By having the students perform these tasks, they are creating their own study guide on the novel and taking responsibility for their learning. All students are given the opportunity to ask questions and get answers. This activity can be repeated more than once during the reading of a novel. You must decide how much time should be spent on questions.

Evaluation

This project can be counted as a class participation activity and thus part of a daily grade. If students are to write more detailed formal responses, it can be considered a writing assignment. The main purpose, however, is to get the students to talk and share information with each other.

Variations

Ask students to choose one of the questions and write a longer, more formal response to it. You can also provide examples of the kinds of questions to ask as a guide for slower students. Students need to practice asking good questions in order to find out the answers.

ACTIVITY 45

SHARE RESPONSES ON A NOVEL

Name: _____ Date: _____

Title: _____

Author: _____

Publisher and year: _____

Directions: Write three questions on individual index cards concerning the plot, characters, universal topics, theme, the relationship of the book to teenagers, problems/solutions, or unusual ideas. Respond to three other students' questions in the boxes below.

Question 1: _____

Name of Person Who Wrote the Question: _____

Answer:

Question 2: _____

Name of Person Who Wrote the Question: _____

Answer:

Question 3: _____

Name of Person Who Wrote the Question: _____

Answer:

ACTIVITY 46

ORAL INTERPRETATION OF A PASSAGE

Purpose of the Activity

This activity focuses primarily on speaking and listening skills. The students must choose a passage from their novel that has a special meaning to them, a significance to the novel, or a strong characterization. Then they must practice it aloud before reading to the class. They must also explain the significance of the passage to the novel and give an explanation for their choice. The audience must practice active listening skills and be nonjudgmental.

How to Use the Activity

This activity involves discussion of the skills necessary for doing a good oral interpretation. The listening skills expected by the audience need to be discussed in class before the presentations begin. Present a couple of readings from literature for the students to hear. Also in preparation, have the students practice their reading with a partner before they make their presentation to the class. You may want to approve the passages first by using the activity worksheet. The time length and length of passage will be set by you.

Evaluation

Both the speakers and listeners may be assessed depending on the maturity of the group. A rubric can be devised to cover the skills being developed. Clarity, volume, speed, eye contact, preparation, time limits, and introductions and conclusions are factors to consider. For the audience, paying attention, not talking, not being a distraction, sitting forward, focusing, taking notes, and responding appropriately are part of a grade.

Variations

Depending on the ability of the group, the students can memorize short passages or poems for their presentation.

ACTIVITY 46

ORAL INTERPRETATION OF A PASSAGE

Name: _____ Date: _____

Title: _____

Author: _____

Publisher and year: _____

Directions: Locate an interesting passage of two or three paragraphs that the class would like to hear read aloud. This passage should also give insight into a character or the theme of the book. Be prepared to explain the significance of your choice and its relationship to the rest of the book. Copy the selection so that it can be submitted at the time of the oral reading.

Page Number of the Passage: _____

Significance of the Passage to the Novel:

Explanation for Your Choice of This Passage:

ACTIVITY 47

SHARE A VOCABULARY WORD A DAY

Purpose of the Activity

There are four purposes for this activity project. The first is to increase the vocabulary of the students by not only having them choose their own words but also teaching the words to each other. Second, through class presentations, the students will practice their speaking skills in front of an audience, relating planned, practiced, and practical information that all classmates need to know. Third, the class members will practice their listening and note-taking skills during the presentations, writing down information on the words that they will later study for a follow-up quiz or activity. Fourth, the students will act appropriately as an audience.

How to Use the Activity

Assign this activity when the students start the novel so they can look for a word to share as they read the pages or chapter assigned. While the book is read and taught, you can spread out the presentations to coincide with the discussion of particular pages or chapters in class. If no more than three or four words are presented at a time, the class time used for this activity is kept to a minimum, and other activities can be planned. You must request that the students take notes, listen attentively, and use the words in future assignments. You might ask students to use the words in compositions and highlight their presence for extra points. The memory aid brought by the students can be objects, actions, or something drawn or written on the chalkboard. These concrete examples will help the audience retain the knowledge of the words.

Evaluation

This activity can be evaluated in several ways: meeting a deadline, following directions for teaching the vocabulary word, content, speaking skills, and audience skill (cooperation, attentiveness, note taking, and behavior). Also, a follow-up quiz or other such activity can assess the students' knowledge of the words.

Variations

Create a list of words if certain ones are necessary for comprehension of the book. Assign each student a word. The student is responsible for presenting information about the word to the class. Students then gain some experience teaching. The words can be divided into pairs or groups, or by books if individuals are reading a variety of novels. The vocabulary map in activity 33 can be used as a guide for the teaching and presenting of the word.

ACTIVITY 47

SHARE A VOCABULARY WORD A DAY

Name: _____ Date: _____

Title: _____

Author: _____

Publisher and year: _____

Directions: Each class member will sign up to present an interesting or unusual vocabulary word from the reading. Class members are expected to take notes on all the presentations. It is your responsibility to teach the word you chose to your classmates. Bring a picture, personal story, or prop to help everyone remember what your word means.

Information Required:

1. Original Sentence and Page Number
2. Part of Speech
3. Definition
4. Your Own Sentence
5. Symbol, Object, Prop, or Other Memory Aid

Name	Page Number	Share Date	Word
1.			
2.			
3.			
4.			
5.			
6.			

From *What a Novel Idea!* © 1997 Katherine Wiesolek Kuta. Teacher Ideas Press. 1-800-237-6124.

Name	Page Number	Share Date	Word
7.			
8.			
9.			
10.			
11.			
12.			
13.			
14.			
15.			
16.			
17.			
18.			
19.			
20.			
21.			

Name	Page Number	Share Date	Word
22.			
23.			
24.			
25.			
26.			
27.			
28.			
29.			
30.			
31.			
32.			
33.			
34.			
35.			

ACTIVITY 48

PANEL DISCUSSION ON A BOOK

Purpose of the Activity

The main purpose of this speaking/listening activity is for students to verbally present multiple points of view on a topic and for class members to listen to their peers' opinions without criticism. The students will practice stating their opinions and supporting them with examples from the books they have completed. The class members will be given an opportunity to question the speakers and to offer comments on what they have heard. Thus, they have the opportunity to practice speaking skills as well.

How to Use the Activity

The students can be divided into groups of four or five for several panel discussion groups, or this activity can be offered as one of several choices for book projects. Either way, there should be one moderator/leader for each group. The group might want to meet to discuss the topics from the book before the actual panel discussion in front of the class. You can choose the number of topics or ideas and set a time limit for the panel discussion when the activity starts. The discussion should be rather informal, with students seated at a table or at desks facing the class members. Each panel member should make a comment about the previous student's statements before any new thoughts or ideas are presented. After each panel member has spoken, the moderator should summarize the points developed for the audience. Then the moderator can receive questions and comments from the audience.

Evaluation

This activity can receive as much credit as other book projects. At the beginning of the activity, the students need to know the criteria being used for evaluation. The panel members can be graded individually for their participation in the panel and their ability to support their opinions with examples from the text. Another assessment can be a group grade for meeting a deadline, working as a group, and completing the speaking project. You can assess the audience's speaking skills as well as the content of their questions or their listening skills.

Variations

A variation of the panel discussion is to control the topics being discussed if the class needs that kind of guidance. Another possibility is for the students to write on index cards the topics that they would like to discuss; each member or panel group can randomly draw one or two topics to deal with.

ACTIVITY 48

PANEL DISCUSSION ON A BOOK

Name: _____Date: _____

Title: _____

Author: _____

Publisher and year: _____

Directions: Each group member is responsible for participating in a panel discussion on the novel when you finish reading it. The panel will come to some conclusions regarding the novel, and the members will individually present them to the class. Each member must have a speaking role, and the others must listen along with the class. At the end of the presentation, class members may ask questions of the group.

Members of Panel (label the moderator):

1. _____
2. _____
3. _____
4. _____
5. _____

Topics of Discussion by Each Member:

1. _____
2. _____
3. _____
4. _____
5. _____

Three to Five General Conclusions About the Novel:

1. _____
2. _____
3. _____
4. _____
5. _____

ACTIVITY 49

RADIO/TELEVISION PUBLICITY SPOT

Purpose of the Activity

This speaking/listening activity allows students to be highly creative in our media-centered world and to learn about advertisement. The students also will experience the process of producing a very precise, concise form of communication through the format of the radio segment or television commercial. The students must work cooperatively if they work in pairs or groups. They must research examples of the format of professionally made radio or television spots. Finally, students are responsible for producing a product for listening or viewing in class.

How to Use the Activity

The availability of equipment at students' homes or at school will be a deciding factor in assigning this type of activity for all students. It can be offered as one of several projects from this book. Before this activity is assigned, students need to discuss advertisements and publicity spots that they have seen to learn about content, appeal, timing, and appearance. Samples can be played in class to use as models. If book promotion is unfamiliar to students, movie advertisements can be talked about and viewed. Another pre-project activity for students is having them listen to a radio play so they become aware of the use of voices, sound effects, and timing. Many young people are unfamiliar with this genre.

Evaluation

The students can be evaluated by the criteria requested in the project and by you. The class can also partake in the evaluation by discussing the strengths and weaknesses of the presentations or by writing down their criticisms and praises.

Variations

The students can work in groups and coordinate this project with other departments in the school district, if available. Perhaps your school has a media specialist, a fine arts department, or staff members who would be willing to help students learn to use special equipment and help them complete the project.

ACTIVITY 49

RADIO/TELEVISION PUBLICITY SPOT

Name: _____ Date: _____

Title: _____

Author: _____

Publisher and year: _____

Directions: Just as television shows and movies advertise their products, books need some advertising. Often, books are promoted in newspapers, in magazines, or at stores. However, you are to create a radio spot on a cassette tape or a television spot on videotape to advertise your book. Your purpose is to try to get others to read the book. The tapes should be no longer than one minute because advertising time is expensive. Your spot must be well planned and well rehearsed before taping.

Here is a list of points to consider:

1. Make sure to give accurate bibliographical information.

2. Tell what kind of book it is so readers know how to locate it in a bookstore or library.

3. Say who would be interested in reading it.

4. Give reasons why someone would want to read the book.

5. Possibly read a short excerpt to catch the reader's interest.

6. State a testimonial of someone who read the book and liked it.

7. If the message is also visual, the appearance of the speaker and the background must be taken into consideration.

8. Make sure to time the piece and listen to it for possible errors.

9. Background music can be used so long as it is not distracting.

10. If the project is going to be done live in front of the class, there can only be one take and one chance for the performance to succeed.

ACTIVITY 50

LIVE INTERVIEW OF NOVEL READERS

Purpose of the Activity

This activity involves several purposes and reading, writing, speaking, and listening standards. Students will read a work of literature in order to express opinions, feelings, and interpretations about it. Students will work in pairs or groups of three or four, cooperatively writing questions to conduct interviews with each other. Another standard of speaking is reinforced through the interview presentations, which are somewhat practiced but performed live in front of an audience of class members. The students in the class will learn how their classmates feel about and interpret a book or author through the interviews, thus practicing their listening skills throughout the presentations.

How to Use the Activity

This activity can be used with a single class novel or with several individual books. You must decide if the interviews are to be paired or in groups for larger classes. A discussion on the process of interviewing should take place when this activity begins because not all students may be aware of the need to write questions that provoke extended responses rather than yes or no answers. The questions should be short and the responses long. The interviewer needs to practice nodding, listening, and asking further in-depth questions of the interviewee. Even though the interviews are rehearsed, the students will do the presentations in a live setting and pretend that they haven't rehearsed so they have more confidence and feel prepared. The activity sheet can be used in the preparation stage and approved by the teacher before the live interview takes place. The same questions can be used by each student for each pair or group.

Evaluation

The activity can be evaluated as a formal presentation in which the entire process is taken into consideration, including preparation time, cooperation with peers, and the speaking presentation of the interview. The audience can be assessed for their behavior and listening skills.

Variations

A variation for this activity that would add spontaneity and make the presentations more impromptu would be to ask the interviewer-interviewee groups to write questions that they can ask other groups. This would eliminate rehearsal time, so the responses would be less well thought out but more natural. Another possibility is for each group to have just one interviewer, with all other students in the group as interviewees. You must set the time limitations and the amount of questioning to be done. This project can be offered as one of several possibilities for students to choose from for a book presentation.

ACTIVITY 50

LIVE INTERVIEW OF NOVEL READERS

Name: _____ Date: _____

Title: _____

Author: _____

Publisher and year: _____

Directions: Present a live interview of one or two people who have read a novel. Although the interview should look unrehearsed, in reality it should be well planned and practiced. The questions should be carefully thought out to cover pertinent information about the book and author. The questions may be approved before the presentation.

Interviewer: _____ **Interviewee:** _____

QUESTION 1

QUESTION 2

QUESTION 3

QUESTION 4

QUESTION 5

QUESTION 6

ACTIVITY 51

ROLE-PLAY AN INTERVIEW WITH AN AUTHOR

Purpose of the Activity

This speaking/listening activity has several purposes. First, the students will learn about the interviewing process by cooperatively researching, preparing, writing, practicing, and presenting a live interview for the class. Second, the students will learn more about the author and the work of literature as they discuss, research, and write questions and answers for the interview. Third, the students will play the roles of interviewer and author. Fourth, the students practice their speaking skills by presenting the interview to the class, and the class practices their listening and audience skills. Fifth, the students use higher thinking skills by drawing conclusions for the class on the information presented.

How to Use the Activity

This activity would work well with a class novel or several independent novels. Students may work in pairs, either assigned or matched because they are reading the same title or author. Students need to be aware of interview techniques, questioning, and responding. Brainstorming or mapping can be used to find out about their prior knowledge of the process. A taped interview can be viewed in class or watched on television as homework. Give class time for students to plan, discuss, and research the project. If this project is offered as one of several choices, the students will be responsible for meeting together. You can set the parameters for questions, length, and depth. The author's biography and picture can be obtained by contacting the publisher or checking with the library.

Evaluation

This project can be assessed as a formal presentation for both individuals. The factors to consider for students are meeting a deadline, being prepared, following directions, having accurate content, using good speaking skills, staying in the role assigned, and informing the class about the novel and author through their choice of questions and answers.

Variations

You can provide materials for research if the ability of the class is very low or the students are young. As an entire class project, the students could be assigned particular authors, or they could randomly draw names of people to present to the class.

ACTIVITY 51

ROLE-PLAY AN INTERVIEW WITH AN AUTHOR

Name: _____ Date: _____

Title: _____

Author: _____

Publisher and year: _____

Directions: You and a partner can imagine that you are interviewing an author of a book. After you do research on the author and carefully rehearse your questions and answers, the class will watch your interview and learn more about the author's background and personality. Make sure information is factual and accurate. There should be at least 10 questions. Think of topics that you wonder most about an author when reading a book. Possible topics are the author's personal life, career, sources of inspiration, purpose for writing, titles of publications, and present status.

Interviewer: _____ **Author:** _____

QUESTION 1
RESPONSE

QUESTION 2
RESPONSE

QUESTION 3

RESPONSE

QUESTION 4

RESPONSE

QUESTION 5

RESPONSE

QUESTION 6

RESPONSE

QUESTION 7

RESPONSE

QUESTION 8

RESPONSE

QUESTION 9

RESPONSE

QUESTION 10

RESPONSE

LIST OF SOURCES

1.

2.

3.

ACTIVITY 52

DRAMATIZE A SCENE

Purpose of the Activity

This speaking/listening activity gives students the opportunity to use their acting and speaking talents. Students must choose an appropriate scene that displays characterization, moves the plot forward, or shows a thematic message. They must work together to plan, organize, rehearse, and perform the scene in the classroom. This project is designed so that students whose learning style is one of action and words will succeed with this form of book project. The members of the class must practice acceptable behavior and active listening skills. The students will learn from each other about the work of literature by hearing the text and dialogue spoken out loud.

How to Use the Activity

To avoid rewriting, students need to choose scenes that contain a great deal of dialogue and very little narration. If you want all your students to act and speak in front of an audience, the class can be divided into groups, and several scenes can be presented. This activity can be offered as one of several choices from this book for a project. The activity sheet can be used to have students organize themselves in the planning stages and can be collected for approval. You will set the time limits for the presentations.

Evaluation

The students can be evaluated in several ways. The total assessment can include the planning sheet, a rough draft of the scene with the parts labeled, how well the students work together, and the final performance. The audience behavior can be assessed as well.

Variations

A more difficult activity would be to have students change the format from a book to a play. Ask students to rewrite a scene and make it all dialogue so that it becomes a mini-play script meant to be acted live. The ability and interests of the students will determine the use, time, and possibilities for this project.

ACTIVITY 52

DRAMATIZE A SCENE

Name: _____ Date: _____

Title: _____

Author: _____

Publisher and year: _____

Directions: Work in groups of _____ and act out a scene from your book that deals with a character, theme, or significant plot episode. Background information may be stated if necessary. The scene should have more dialogue than narration, and the lines should be memorized if possible. The scene should be approximately _____ minutes in length.

Group Members:

Name of Scene and Page Number:

Significance of Scene to the Book:

Reason for Choosing This Scene:

Narrator, Characters, and Their Descriptions:

1. _____

2. _____

3. _____

4. _____

Short Summary of Plot Episode:

Props, Sets, or Costumes Needed:

ACTIVITY 53

THUMBS UP/THUMBS DOWN BOOK REVIEW

Purpose of Activity

This higher-level thinking activity involves both speaking and listening standards. Students must make judgments on several elements of the book and discuss them with the class. Not only must they form opinions, but they must also support these opinions with specific examples from the text. Students will practice their speaking skills with an audience while the audience practices listening to their peers' opinions and deciding if they agree or disagree.

How to Use the Activity

This activity can be used with students reading a variety of selections so they can listen to the book reviews and decide which books they would like to read. If all the students have read the same book, they can listen to their classmates' opinions on it. The students can discuss what kinds of elements should be considered for the book reviews. Sample book or movie reviews can be used as examples to build the students' prior knowledge. Time can be given in class for students to look for one to three examples from the text to support their opinions. The time limitation for the presentation should be stated at the onset of the project.

Evaluation

This formal presentation can be assessed according to the presentation of judgments about elements of the novel with adequate support from the text. Speaking skills, meeting a deadline, organization, and knowledge of the text are other factors to consider. The audience can also be assessed for listening skills.

Variations

You can require a visual chart of the information being presented and support passages to be quoted directly rather than simply cited. Students can write an overall summary of what was presented.

ACTIVITY 53

THUMBS UP/THUMBS DOWN BOOK REVIEW

Name: _____ Date: _____

Title: _____

Author: _____

Publisher and year: _____

Directions: Give a short book review on five 🖐 aspects of the novel using the symbols of 👍 for "thumbs up," which signifies a positive point, and 👎 for "thumbs down," which signifies a negative point. All opinions must be explained, and specific examples from the text must be used for support. The chart below can be used as a guide.

Element of Book Being Critiqued	👍 👎	Why?
1.	👍 👎	
2.	👍 👎	
3.	👍 👎	
4.	👍 👎	
5.	👍 👎	

ACTIVITY 54

IMAGERY/FIGURATIVE LANGUAGE PRESENTATION

Purpose of the Activity

The primary purpose of this activity is for students to show their understanding of imagery and figurative language as used by an author. Students must understand the terms and look for examples from the text in order to share lines, passages, and literal meanings with their peers. The students will practice their speaking skills, and the class will practice active listening skills by participating as an audience.

How to Use the Activity

This activity can be used with an entire class, or it can be offered as one of several choices from this book. The literary terms should be taught, discussed, and practiced, possibly with poetry, before this activity is assigned with a novel. Students need to become familiar with these devices before they can look for them in a larger work. The worksheet can be used as a rough draft before a presentation. By having students read their findings aloud, the whole class hears the author's picturesque language. Students can work in pairs to help each other figure out the literal meanings of the figurative language.

Evaluation

Depending on your purpose, this activity can be assessed as a class assignment or as a formal presentation. If it is used as a formal speaking presentation, then before their presentations, students must practice the words from the text and their explanations for the meanings of the quotes. Speaking skills such as eye contact, clarity, articulation, enunciation, and volume are all important parts of a presentation.

Variations

This activity can be used for students to practice locating stylistic writing devices. Students can write their own imagery and figurative language in the boxes and even use these devices in their future papers.

ACTIVITY 54

IMAGERY/FIGURATIVE LANGUAGE PRESENTATION

Name: _____ Date: _____

Title: _____

Author: _____

Publisher and year: _____

Directions: Locate specific forms of imagery and figurative language that the author used in the novel to create word pictures, descriptions, and a style of writing. Copy the lines from the text in the correct category and explain the meaning of the figurative language because it means more than what is literally stated. Make sure you include the page number.

Be prepared to share a sample with the class in an oral presentation.

Simile—A comparison using "like" or "as"

Metaphor—A comparison not using "like" or "as"

Personification—Giving human traits to nonliving objects

Hyperbole—An exaggeration

Onomatopoeia—Words that resemble the sounds

Alliteration—Two or more words that have the same initial sound

Imagery—Words that create "visual" word pictures

Imagery—Words that create "sound" word pictures

Imagery—Words that create "taste" word pictures

Imagery—Words that create "touch" word pictures

Imagery—Words that create "smell" word pictures

ACTIVITY 55

CREATE AND SHARE A CHILDREN'S BOOK

Purpose of the Activity

This activity combines all the standards of reading, writing, representing, viewing, speaking, and listening. First, the students will finish a novel and must understand its overall theme or message. Second, they must show their understanding of the theme and of the parts of a story by writing their own children's book containing the same or a similar theme. Third, they will represent the meaning of each page of the story by illustrating it with symbolic pictures. Fourth, they will share their books with the class by reading them aloud and displaying the illustrations. Fifth, by reading their books aloud and explaining how they used the theme from the novel, they will practice speaking skills. Sixth, the audience will practice listening skills and gain a greater understanding of universal themes and the elements of fictional stories.

How to Use the Activity

This activity can be assigned to all members of a class, or it can be offered as one of several projects after a novel is finished. Before this project is assigned, students should read several children's books to learn about the elements of fiction such as plot, characters, setting, mood, theme, and point of view. After evaluating the qualities of a good book, they need to find these elements in the novels that they read. Then they will go through the process of prewriting, outlining, drafting, revising, rewriting, editing, and doing a final draft. At the end, students can work on illustrations before sharing their books with others. Class time can be used for students to write and also to help edit their classmates' work.

Evaluation

This formal project can be assessed according to all the standards listed above. The students should be told the assessment process at the onset of the project, especially any areas that you want them to concentrate on more heavily.

Variations

Offer the students the opportunity to read their stories not only to their peers but also to lower elementary students or preschool students. Older students take great pride in their work if it is appreciated in a real setting.

ACTIVITY 55

CREATE AND SHARE A CHILDREN'S BOOK

Name: _____ Date: _____

Title: _____

Author: _____

Publisher and year: _____

Directions: Create a children's book with a theme (message) similar to the one you have just finished. Use the form on the next page to design and lay out the book. Copy as many pages as needed to complete your book. The interior square should be used for writing (text) and the exterior squares should be for illustrations, symbols, or colors that enhance the meaning of the page. Several pages will be needed to form a book.

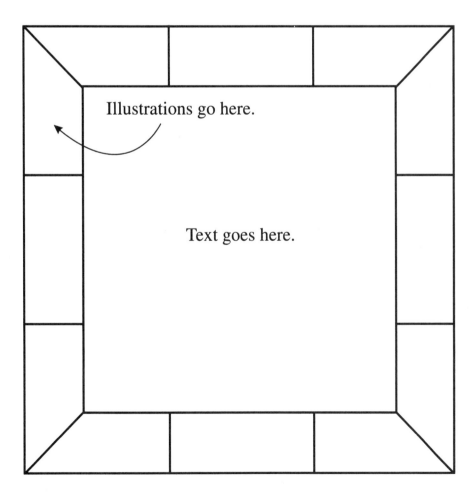

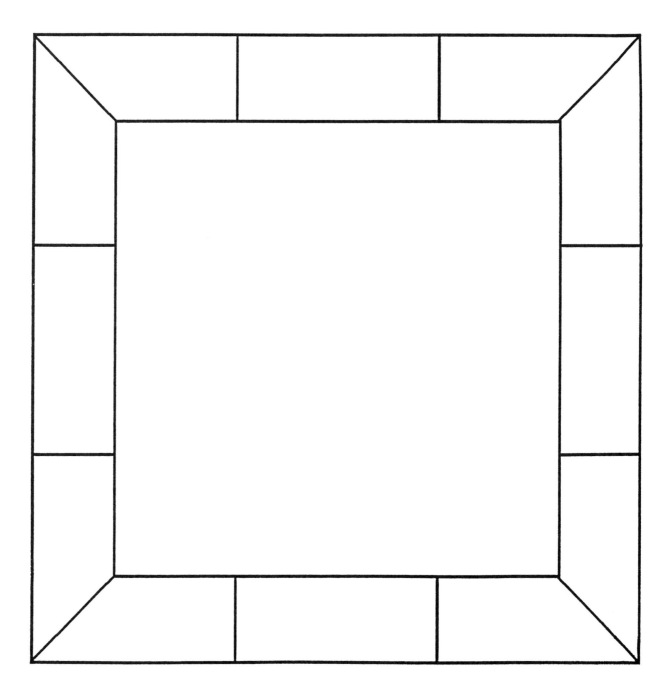

ACTIVITY 56

SHARING AN ACROSTIC POEM MADE FROM THE TITLE

Purpose of the Activity

This activity involves writing, speaking, and listening standards. Students will write a creative poem based on the title of a work of literature. They will show their own meanings and feelings through their interpretation. The students must also illustrate the purpose or idea of the poem. The students will share their own poem with the class in an oral reading. Afterwards, to increase the students' self-esteem, the poems can be displayed in the classroom either on a bulletin board or as a booklet containing the entire class's poems. The booklets can be photocopied, stapled, and given to each class member.

How to Use the Activity

Because the formula for writing an acrostic is very simple, all students can succeed at this fun activity. It can be used for a class novel or individual works and can be used as a class activity rather than a take-home book project. Students can create their poems by hand or on a computer. Sharing can either be formal or informal. You must decide the purpose of the activity and make the students aware of its value.

Evaluation

This activity can be assessed as a class activity, homework assignment, or book project depending on the level, age, and maturity of the students.

Variations

Students enjoy making acrostics out of their names, cities, characters' names, vocabulary, and other words significant to them. This form of poetry can be used as an introduction to standard poetry. Sometimes this kind of poem is useful as a memory cue for remembering words or details.

ACTIVITY 56

SHARING AN ACROSTIC POEM MADE FROM THE TITLE

Name: _____ Date: _____

Title: _____

Author: _____

Publisher and year: _____

Directions: The creative portion of this assignment is to write an acrostic poem using the letters of the title from the book that you have finished. This form of poetry is usually unrhymed. The title of the book is written vertically. Each letter of the title starts a new line, and each line may be a word, phrase, or short sentence that starts with the letter that heads the line (see below). Illustrations around the poem would make it more attractive. The poem can be about anything related to the book or your own personal feelings about the subject matter or theme. The sharing portion of this assignment will be the oral presentation of the poem to the class.

This

Is

The

Lovely

Example

ACTIVITY 57

IMPROMPTU RESPONSE SPEECHES

Purpose of the Activity

This speaking/listening activity gives students the opportunity to practice thinking in a short amount of time, which is a necessary life skill. Students must organize their thoughts quickly to present a short response based on a just-completed novel. They must use specific examples from the reading to support their opinions. Finally, they will practice their speaking skills in front of an audience while the audience practices listening skills.

How to Use the Activity

This class activity is most successful after a novel has been read, either by the class or by individuals. The response questions should be cut up and placed in a container so students can randomly draw one to respond to in an impromptu speech. The speeches can be timed so that all students have an opportunity to speak in the same class period. Either before or after the speeches, you can discuss the necessity of learning the useful life skill of thinking on one's feet.

Evaluation

This activity can be assessed in terms of participation, answering the chosen response, and speaking skills. The amount of credit for the activity depends on your purpose and the level of the class. One possibility is simply to offer students an "A" for completing the response presentation or a "0" for choosing not to participate.

Variations

Students can write their own questions that they would like answered about the book, and impromptu speeches can be used with any type of literature.

ACTIVITY 57

IMPROMPTU RESPONSE SPEECHES

Name: _____ Date: _____

Title: _____

Author: _____

Publisher and year: _____

Directions: You will pick a question about the book you just read from a bag. You will then have two minutes to prepare an impromptu answer to the question. Use specific examples in your response to explain your generalizations.

Questions in the Bag:

1. What does the title of the book mean to the plot and to the readers?

2. What came as a surprise to you in the book and why?

3. In what ways are you like any of the characters? Explain.

4. What was the best part of the book and why?

5. Whom would you recommend this book to and why?

6. Was there a character that reminds you of a real person you know? Explain how the two people are similar.

7. Did you like the ending of the book? Why or why not?

8. What connections can you make between the book and your life? Explain.

9. What do you predict will happen after the ending? Explain.

10. What character would you like to be or not be? Why?

11. What actor would you choose to play the role of the main character? Why?

12. What song would you choose to use as a theme song for this book? Why?

13. What message in the book is relevant to all people? Explain.

14. Is this book believable (could the events have happened in real life)? Why or why not?

15. Is there a character that you would like to have as a friend? Who? Why?

16. What was your strongest feeling while reading the book, and what caused this emotion? Explain.

17. What questions would you like to ask the author if you had the opportunity? Why?

18. What confused you in the book? Why?

19. What was the main issue of the book and how is it relevant in young people's lives? Explain.

20. What are five adjectives that describe the main character? Explain why you chose these descriptive words.

21. What was the setting of the book and where have you been that reminded you of this setting?

22. What was ironic or surprising to you in some way? Explain.

23. Was there a person who could be considered a hero for some reason? Explain why or why not.

24. Is there a movie that reminds you of this book in some way? Explain.

25. What was the problem and solution in the book? Did you agree or disagree with the decision? Explain.

ACTIVITY 58

MOOD TALKS

Purpose of the Activity

This speaking and listening activity has students speak in front of their classmates after being given only a short time to prepare. This forces students to learn to think quickly, form opinions, organize what they have to say, and support their opinions with examples from the text. The class members will practice listening skills and audience behavior. By using common feelings and emotions, the speakers reinforce their knowledge about the mood created by the author to get readers emotionally involved in the text.

How to Use the Activity

This activity would be most successful as a post-reading class activity. Students enjoy randomly drawing their assignments rather than being given specific ones, so cut the chart into pieces and put them into a box or hat. You can also have them draw numbers to determine the order of their presentations. After students draw their slips of paper, you can decide how long they have to prepare their speeches and how many examples should be given from the text possibly by using the brainstorming sheet on page 137. Students may need to look in the text for support for their responses. A good time limit for the presentations is one minute each.

Evaluation

This speaking activity can be assessed as other speeches have been. Students should be aware from the beginning what the evaluation process will include. Speaking elements such as clarity, loudness, pacing, and eye contact can be factors in the evaluation. The audience can be evaluated in terms of attentiveness and appropriate behavior.

Variations

This activity can be used to teach or review moods with any kind of literature. Whenever an activity can be made into a game, the students are more eager to participate and the chances for success increase. In this vein, have students think of situations from one or several pieces of literature and write them down on cards. Then randomly draw the cards and ask the students to match them to the emotions and feelings on the sheet. The first student to get a predetermined number of matches correct is the winner and receives extra points.

ACTIVITY 58

MOOD TALKS

Name: _____ Date: _____

Title: _____

Author: _____

Publisher and year: _____

Directions: Choose a feeling, emotion, or mood common to all people. In a set amount of time, you will prepare a short speech explaining the meaning of the term and give a couple of examples when the emotion was displayed by a character in the novel, or when you felt it because of an event or situation. The examples must be specific.

ANGER	DEPRESSION	EXCITEMENT	DETERMINATION
SADNESS	HAPPINESS	STRESS	PERSEVERANCE
SUSPENSE	CONFUSION	JEALOUSY	MYSTERY
DESPAIR	ANXIETY	RELIEF	EXHAUSTION
TENDERNESS	DEPENDENCE	ARROGANCE	EMPATHY
BELLIGERENCE	CLOSE-MINDEDNESS	OPENNESS	FRUSTRATION
CAPABLE	COMFORTABLE	DISAPPOINTMENT	ISOLATION

From *What a Novel Idea!* © 1997 Katherine Wiesolek Kuta. Teacher Ideas Press. 1-800-237-6124.

Brainstorming Sheet

Use this form to organize your ideas and prepare your talk.

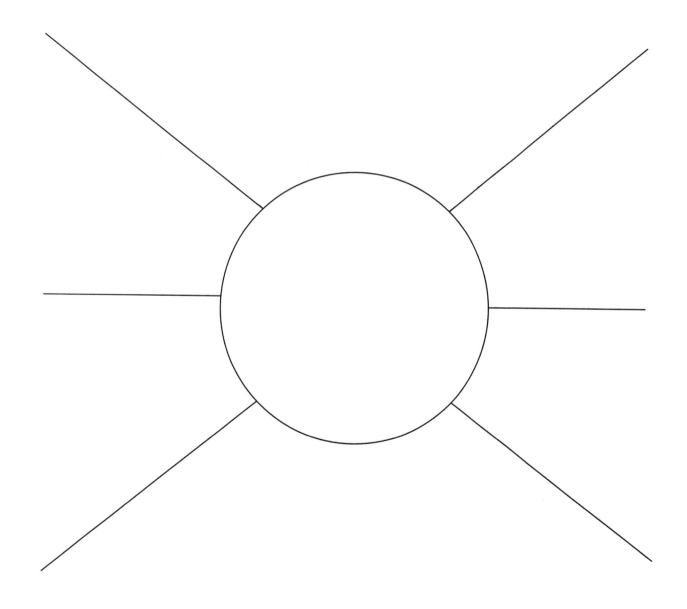

ACTIVITY 59

CREATE A GAME ABOUT A NOVEL

Purpose of the Activity

Although this activity involves some writing skills, the emphasis is on speaking and listening skills and cooperative learning. Students must work together to create a board game based on an aspect of the novel. They must not only design the game's format but also create the rules, questions, answers, and ways of winning. Then they will share their game with the class or other groups and play it. Students will learn from each other as they discuss various aspects of the novel, such as vocabulary, characters, plot directions, or themes. Students take turns reading and speaking the questions. The other students can practice listening skills as they participate.

How to Use the Activity

Students can be divided into groups so that all members are working on the same project at the same time but creating different games. Another possibility is to offer this project as one of several choices from this book so that students interested in this type of creative endeavor can undertake this project. If all students are working on group games, then groups may want to take turns playing each other's creations. The games should be simple enough for all class members to play, yet contain informational elements so that they are a learning device. Before game creation starts, discuss the students' favorite games and what elements are necessary for a good board game. Because students are often more familiar with computer games than board games, board games should be brought into the classroom to display the board, directions, pieces, and accessories.

Evaluation

This project can be assessed as a creative project would be in terms of meeting a deadline, originality, creativity, information, organization, and practicality. The students can be evaluated on their cooperative working and their game-playing participation.

Variations

You can control both the type of game to be created and the topics that the game covers. Place the topics on index cards and have each group randomly draw one that their game will be based on. Possible topics include character traits, quotations, solving a mystery, historical background, themes, vocabulary, plot decisions, and comparing and contrasting several works of literature.

ACTIVITY 59

CREATE A GAME ABOUT A NOVEL

Name: _____ Date: _____

Title: _____

Author: _____

Publisher and year: _____

Directions: Create a simple board game based on one aspect of the novel using the activity form or devising one of your own. Some possibilities include: vocabulary, characters, plot, and theme. Use this page for planning.

Title of Game: _____

Purpose of Game: _____

_____

_____

Directions: _____

_____

_____

_____

_____

Rules: _____

_____

_____

_____

_____

_____

ACTIVITY 60

PRESENTING BUTTONS AND T-SHIRT

Purpose of the Activity

There are several purposes for this activity. The first is to have the students think, write, and create nontraditional communication forms such as message buttons and T-shirts, which can contain important universal messages. Second, the students will promote both their novels and the pleasure of reading in their messages. Third, by having the students present their buttons and T-shirt designs to the class along with an explanation for their creations, they can be proud of their work. Fourth, the audience will practice listening skills.

How to Use the Activity

This activity can be done by an entire class or given as one of several for students to choose from for their project and presentation. Discuss the ideas of universal themes and marketing approaches used when trying to promote a product. Several examples of buttons, T-shirts, cups, magnets, and other promotional items can be brought in as examples. As space is limited, word choice and catchy, clever sayings become very significant. Students can work together or individually in brainstorming before or during the project. Artwork, color, and design are issues that an art teacher can speak to the class about or that can be researched.

There are two buttons on the activity page because one is to promote the novel and the other the idea of reading for enjoyment. The T-shirt design can be enlarged for more effect. After students present the projects to the class, the items can be displayed in the classroom.

Evaluation

This activity can be assessed informally or formally depending on whether it is a class activity or a formal book project. Originality, creativity, appearance, content of message, and explanation of the message in relationship to the novel are all factors to consider. Students in the audience will be graded on listening skills and appropriate audience behavior.

Variations

Once the buttons and T-shirts are created, you can laminate them for safekeeping. Students can draw or create on a computer many other objects that can be used for promotion, such as hats, belts, candy bars, kites, or billboards.

ACTIVITY 60

PRESENTING BUTTONS AND T-SHIRT

Name: _____ Date: _____

Title: _____

Author: _____

Publisher and year: _____

Directions: Brainstorm possible universal messages or sayings that could apply to both your novel and the reading you do for pleasure. Then narrow your choices to create two buttons. One button should refer to your novel and the other reading. The buttons should be creative, decorative, and original.

Because a T-shirt design allows more space for a message or advertisement, create a T-shirt to promote either the novel or your pleasure reading.

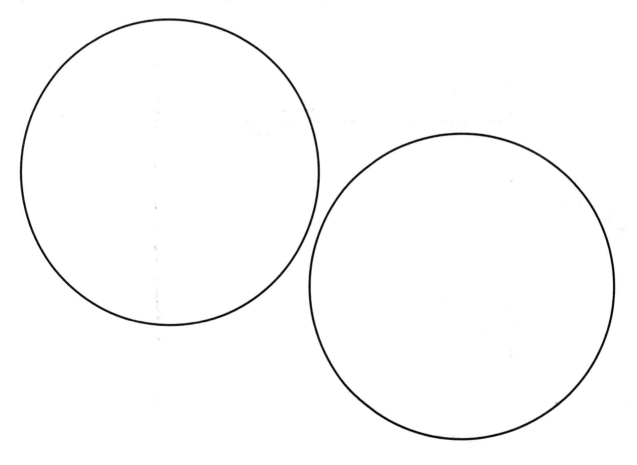

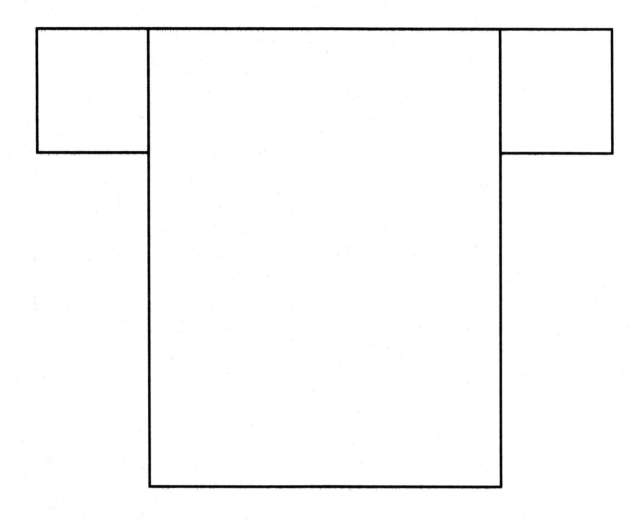

ABOUT THE AUTHOR

Katherine Kuta lives in a northwest suburb of Chicago, Illinois, with her husband and four-year-old daughter. She has been teaching for more than twenty years, from kindergarten through college level but has spent the majority of her career teaching high school. At present she teaches English and is a Reading Specialist at Maine East High School in Park Ridge, Illinois. She is active in several professional organizations and often works with teachers in staff development and speaks to educators. Through meeting young adult authors and reading young adult literature grew the desire to write and share ideas on successful teaching. In addition to teaching, reading, and writing, Katherine likes to spend time traveling, snow skiing, playing tennis, and riding horses. Katherine believes that books and activities *for* young people and *about* young people give them experiences about others and helps them understand the world they live in a little better.